Practice Book

Grade 1

Harcourt School Publishers

www.harcourtschool.com

Printed in the United States of America

ISBN 10: 0-15-349872-2
ISBN 13: 978-0-15-349872-5

20 0868 15 14 13 4500407649

Contents

Spring Forward—Book 1-1

Zoom Along—Book 1-2

REACH FOR THE STARS—BOOK 1-3

Watch This!—Book 1-5

Spring Forward

Book 1-1

Name ____________________

▶ Circle the word that names the picture. Then write the word.

1. 

sad
cat
hat

2. 

rag
bag
tan

3. 

fan
man
fat

4. 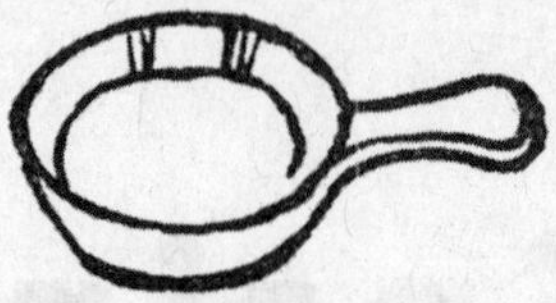

ran
pad
pan

5. 

nap
ham
jam

6. 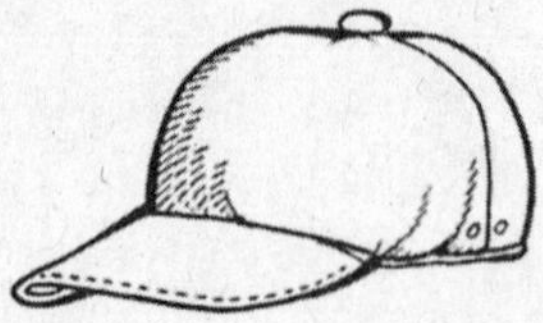

sag
can
cap

7. 

man
ran
wax

8. 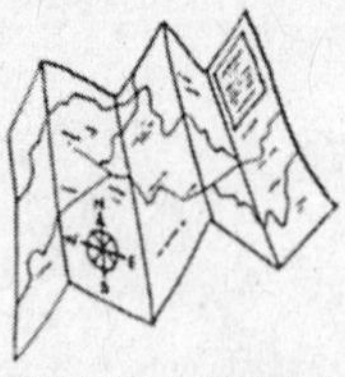

tap
map
mad

School-Home Connection

Have your child read each word aloud. Ask her or him to choose two words and say them in a sentence.

Name ____________________

Read the Spelling Words. Then write each word in the group where it belongs.

Spelling Words

- am
- at
- cat
- can
- ran
- man
- map
- tap
- a
- the

Words with a

Word without a

School-Home Connection

Have your child read each Spelling Word aloud. Talk about how the words are alike and how they are different.

Name ______________________

▶ **Circle the word that completes each sentence. Then write the word.**

mat hat

1. Jan has a ________.

fan nap

2. Max had a ________.

ran sat

3. Pam ________.

lad sad

4. I am ________.

cat can

5. He has a ________.

School-Home Connection

Have your child read the words and sentences aloud. Ask him or her to write other words with the short *a* sound.

Name ______________________

Write the word that best completes each sentence.

man	now	mad

1. Max can bat ____________.

help	ham	hat

2. Dad can ____________ Max.

Lap	Let's	Lab

3. ____________ see Max go!

School-Home Connection

Have your child read each sentence aloud. Ask your child to say these words in other sentences: *now, help, let's.*

Name ______________________________

Read the sentences. Draw a line from the sentences to the picture that shows what will happen next.

1. Jan can bat.
She can bat now.

2. I have a rag.
I go to the van.

3. Pat ran.
Pat ran a lap.

School-Home Connection
Ask your child to read the sentences to you. Then have your child predict what might happen next.

Name ______________________________

Write the word that completes the sentence.

1. Dan has ________.   cat / cats

2. I see two ________.   bat / bats

3. Jan ________ Max.   tag / tags

4. The cat ________.   nap / naps

5. There are two ________.   van / vans

School-Home Connection

Have your child read the words and sentences aloud to you.

Name ________________

Add words to make each word or group of words into a sentence. Write the sentences correctly.

1. ran

2. we

3. the cat

4. i like

5. has

School-Home Connection

Have your child create sentences about things he or she can do, and say them aloud. Ask your child to tell how to begin and end each sentence.

Name ____________________

Circle the word that completes the sentence. Then write the word.

map tap

1. Pam can ____________.

tags wags

2. Jan ____________ Dan.

raps ran

3. The cat ____________ out.

can pan

4. I want that ____________.

am at

5. I ____________ a cat.

School-Home Connection

Have your child read each sentence aloud. Ask which words have the short *a* sound as in *van*.

Name ______________________________

▶ **Read the Spelling Words. Then write each word in the group where it belongs.**

Spelling Words

hat
had
sad
sat
bat
bag
at
can
help
now

Words with a

______________ ______________

______________ ______________

______________ ______________

______________ ______________

______________ ______________

______________ ______________

______________ ______________

______________ ______________

Words without a

______________ ______________

School-Home Connection

Ask your child to change the last letter in the word *hat* to make another Spelling Word (*had*). Repeat this activity with the words *sad* (*sat*) and *bat* (*bag*).

Name ______________________

▶ Write the word from the box that completes each sentence

sad	ran	cat	can

1. I see a ________.

2. Pat has a ________.

3. She ________.

4. I am ________.

School–Home Connection

Have your child read the word choices and each sentence aloud. Talk about what is happening in the pictures.

Name ______________________________

▶ Write the word that best completes the sentence.

an in up

1. I look ________ the pan.

no nap do

2. I see ________ ham.

tap tan too

3. I want ham, ________.

School–Home Connection

Have your child read each word and sentence aloud. Encourage your child to write the words *in*, *no*, and *too* in other sentences.

Name ______________________________

Read the story. Look at the picture. Circle the sentence that tells what will happen next.

1. My cat ran to me.
My cat sat in my lap.

My cat has a nap. My cat looks at a van.

2. Jan looks at a map.
Pam sat down.

Pam ran out. Pam looks at the map.

3. I have two bats.
Dan wants a bat.

I give Dan one bat. Dan gives me a bat.

School-Home Connection
Have your child read the sentences aloud. Talk about how the pictures relate to the words. Ask your child what else could happen next based on the story.

Name ______________________

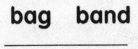

Circle the word that completes the sentence. Then write the word.

bag band

____

1. I am in a ____________.

tag hand

____

2. I see the ____________.

wag and

____

3. Max ____________ Nan are fans.

sag sand

____

4. She sat in the ____________.

rag land

____

5. Give me that ____________.

School-Home Connection

Ask your child to read each sentence aloud. Then ask him or her to find the words on the page that rhyme with *bag*. (tag, wag, sag, rag)

Name

▶ **Write each sentence correctly.**

1. down cat the sat

2. had nap a he

3. in rat a ran

▶ **Write a sentence that tells what happens next.**

4.

School-Home Connection

Make up simple sentences that use no more than four words. Then say each sentence with the words out of order. Ask your child to say the sentence correctly.

Name ____________________

▶ **Circle the word that names each picture. Then write the word.**

1. 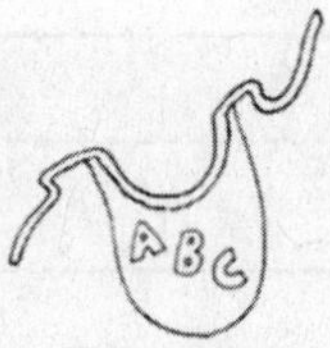

bib
bag
bit

2. 

wag
win
wig

3. 

pad
pit
pig

4. 

sax
six
silk

5. 

hat
hit
him

6. 

lips
laps
limps

7. 

pill
pan
pin

8. 

lad
lid
lift

School-Home Connection

Point to each word with *i* on this page. Ask your child to read the word. Then have him or her say it in a sentence.

Name ______________________

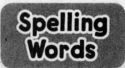

▶ **Read the Spelling Words. Then write each word in the group where it belongs.**

Words with i

______________ ______________

______________ ______________

______________ ______________

______________ ______________

______________ ______________

Words without i

______________ ______________

______________ ______________

Spelling Words

in
pin
pig
big
dig
did
had
sat
no
too

School-Home Connection

Write the word *pig* and have your child change one letter to make another Spelling Word. (*big, dig, pin*)

Name ______________________________

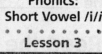

Cross out the word that is wrong.
Write the correct word.

1. My hat is too bag.

2. This hat will fat.

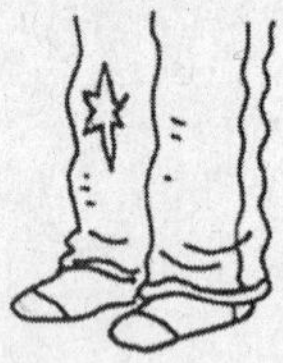

3. My pants have a rap.

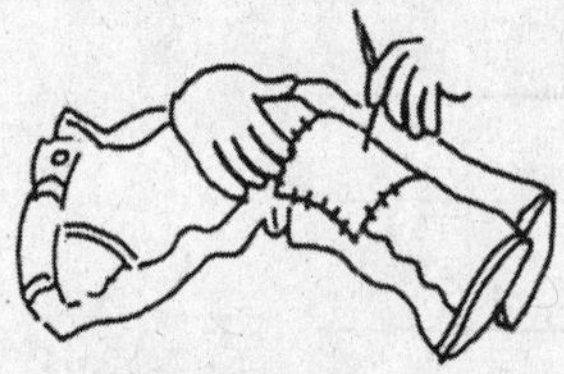

4. This will fax it.

5. He ran and had.

6. I ran to ham.

School-Home Connection

Read each sentence with the incorrect word. Ask your child to listen carefully, and then read the sentence with the correct word.

Name ________________________________

Read the sentences. Write the contraction for the underlined words.

Where's	What's	He's
Here's	That's	It's

1. Here is the gift.

2. It is a hat.

3. Where is Dan?

4. He is here now.

5. What is that?

6. That is a gift for you.

School-Home Connection

Say a simple sentence with one of the contractions above. Then ask your child what two words go together to make the contraction.

Name ________________________________

▶ Add a naming part from the box to complete each sentence.

Liz	We	I	Dan

1. __________ will go on a raft.

2. __________ can help lift it.

3. __________ has a map.

4. __________ get on.

▶ Write a sentence that tells what happens next. Write your sentence correctly. Then circle the naming part.

5. ____

School-Home Connection

Draw a picture with your child. Have your child use complete sentences to tell you what is happening in the picture. Then ask, "Who or what is the sentence about?"

Name ______________________________

Write the words where they belong in the puzzle.

call	wall	fall	ball

1. 

2. 

3. 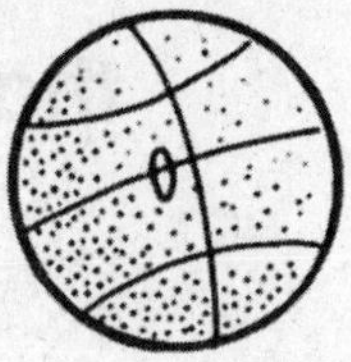

4. 

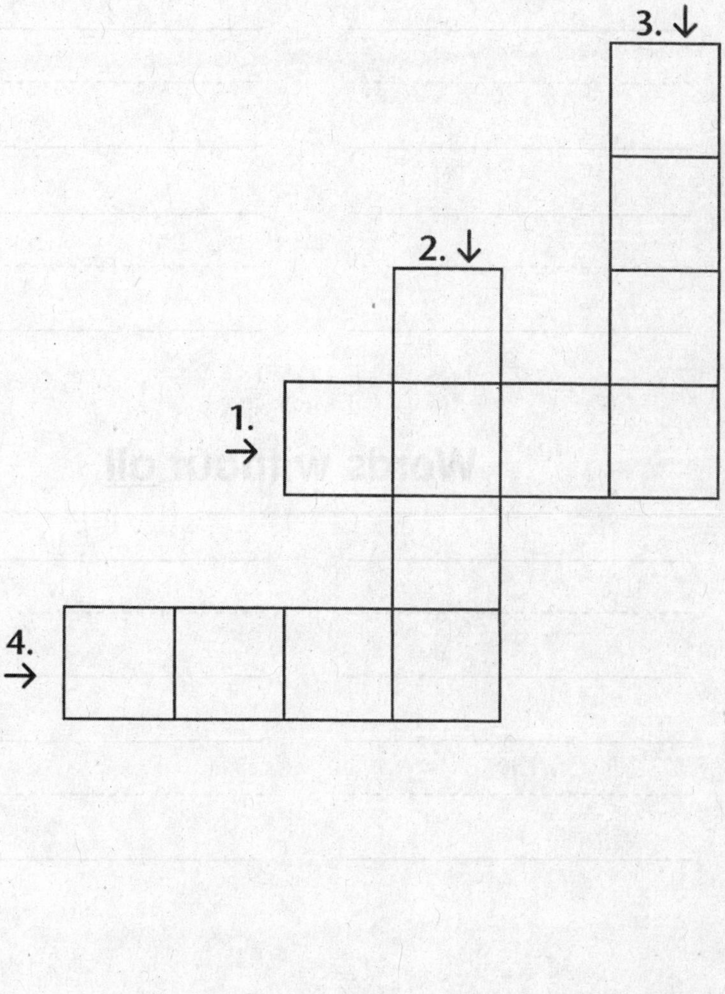

School-Home Connection

Write the words *hall*, *mall*, and *tall*. Say a clue for each word and have your child point to the correct word.

Practice Book

Name ______________________________

▶ **Read the Spelling Words. Then write each word in the group where it belongs.**

Spelling Words

all
call
fall
wall
ball
tall
not
top
much
thank

Words with all

______________ ______________

______________ ______________

______________ ______________

Words without all

______________ ______________

______________ ______________

School–Home Connection

Have your child read the first six Spelling Words aloud. Then use those words to make rhyming sentences.

Name ______________________________

Circle the word that completes each sentence. Then write the word.

ball **bill**

1. Dad kicks the ____________ to Max.

hall **hill**

2. Max kicks it down the ____________.

fall **fill**

3. Do not ____________, Max!

wall **will**

4. Now Jan ____________ kick the ball.

all **ill**

5. They ____________ ran fast to get it.

School-Home Connection

Have your child read each completed sentence aloud. Talk about how the word choices are alike and how they are different.

Name ______________________

Write the word that best completes the sentence.

out of fox

1. This is a map ________ the mall.

sand make some

2. I want to get ________ pants.

Hop How Had

3. ________ do they fit?

milk make miss

4. Mom will ________ them fit.

School-Home Connection

Have your child read each completed sentence aloud. Point to the words *of, some, How,* and *make*. Ask your child to say each word in another sentence.

Pam and Cat

1

Cat ran.

3

Here, Cat! Look!

6

Pam pats Cat.

8

Fold

Fold

2 Look!

Come down, Cat! 7

Fold

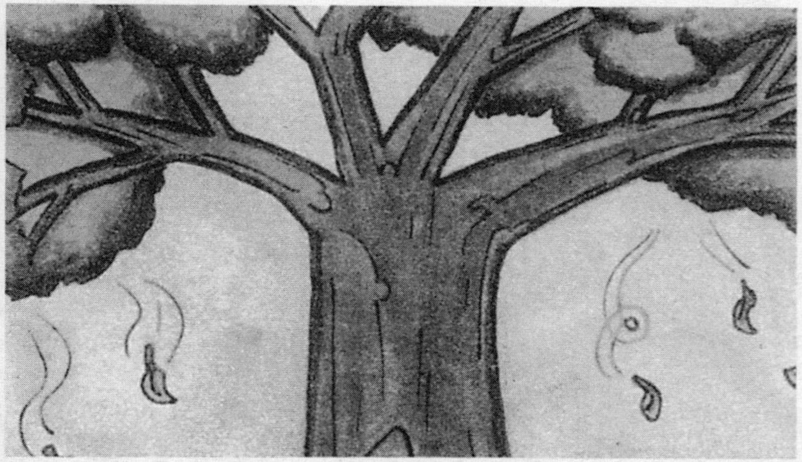

4 Now where is Cat?

Come down, Cat! 5

Dan and Sam

1

We like to tap.

3

6

Dan and Sam are down!

8

No! Dan and Sam are pals.

Fold

Fold

2 Can you tap, Dan?

Are Dan and Sam mad? 7

4 Dan sat. Sam sat, too.

Dan and Sam ran. 5

Fold

Fold

It's Max! It's Ann!

Max and Ann are here!

8

Ann and Max

1

Fold

6

Ann is here.

Ann can go.

3

Fold

2 Max can go.

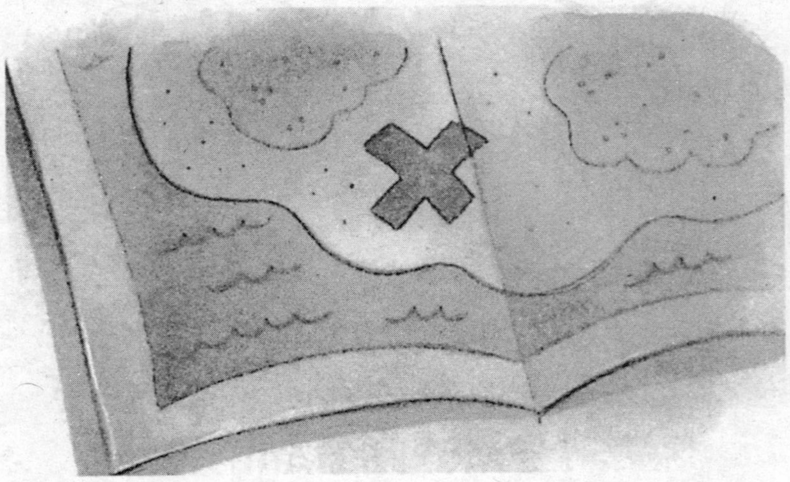

They can get here soon. 7

Fold

Fold

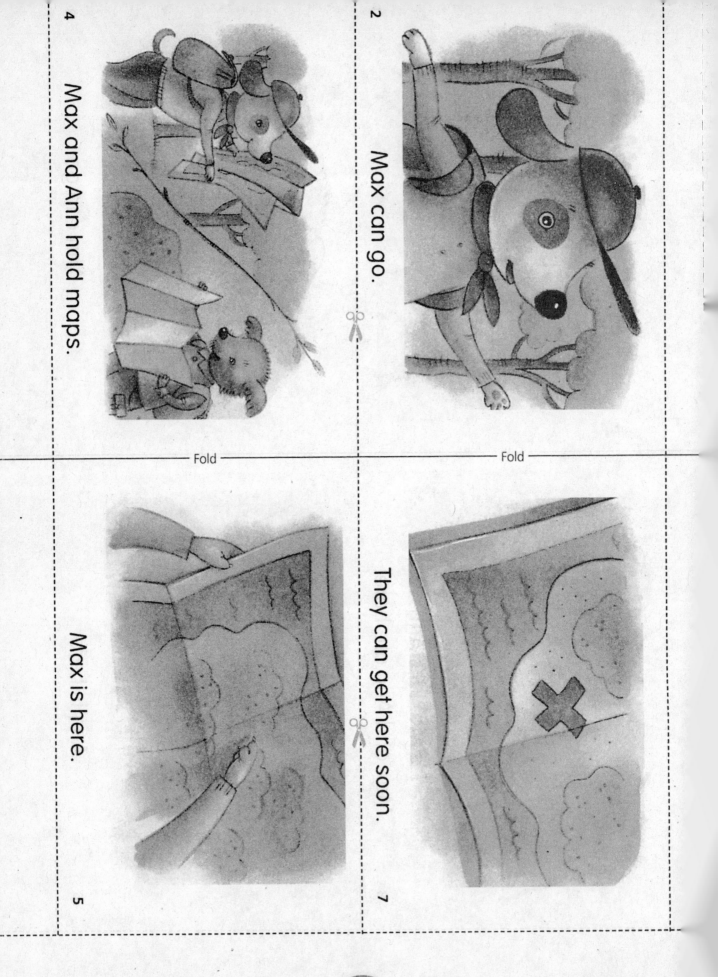

4 Max and Ann hold maps.

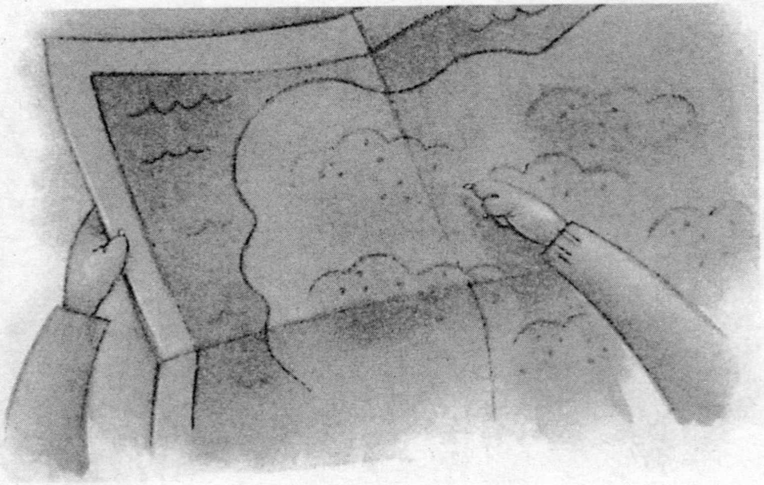

Max is here. 5

Jack and Sid

1

Look at what I have, Jack. 3

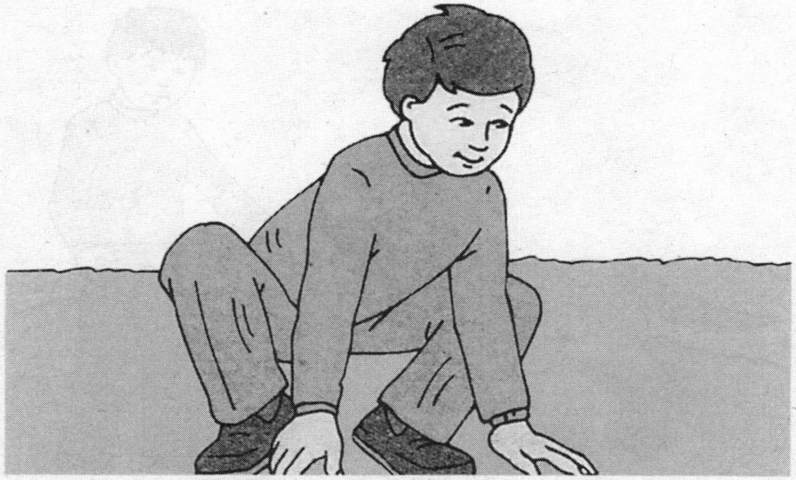

6 I will help. Sit like I do, Jack.

8 Yes! Sid pats him on the back.

Fold

Fold

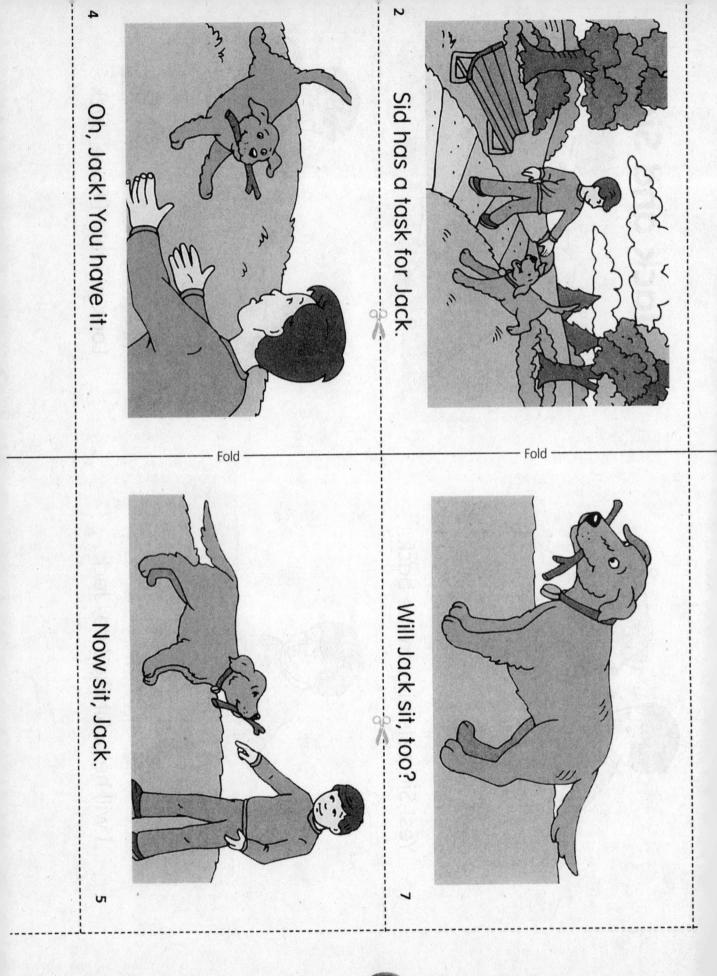

Sid has a task for Jack.

2

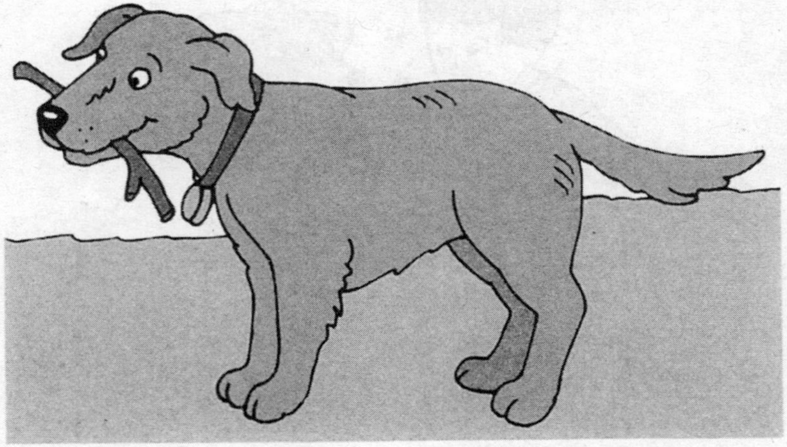

Will Jack sit, too?

7

Fold

Oh, Jack! You have it.

4

Now sit, Jack.

5

Fold

What Is In It?

1

Tim's sack is big, too.
Will he find rocks in it?

3

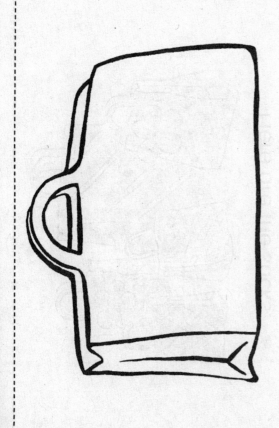

Jan has sacks.
The sacks have dots.

6

What is in it?

8

Fold

Fold

Liz's sack is big.
What can fit in it?

2

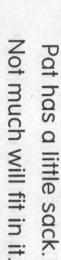

Here are the sacks.
Pick the sack for you.

7

Fold

Pat has a little sack.
Not much will fit in it.

4

The dog has a sack, too.
Dogs do not pack sacks!

5

Fold

Thank You, Mom!

1

Where did they all go?

3

6 I see the box here.

8 That's how I got it!

Fold

Fold

2 Look up on that hill.

Mom will help me get one! 7

Fold

4 A tall man picked some.

He packed some in a box. 5

Fold

The Lost Dog

Characters

Ann

Tim

Dad

Mom

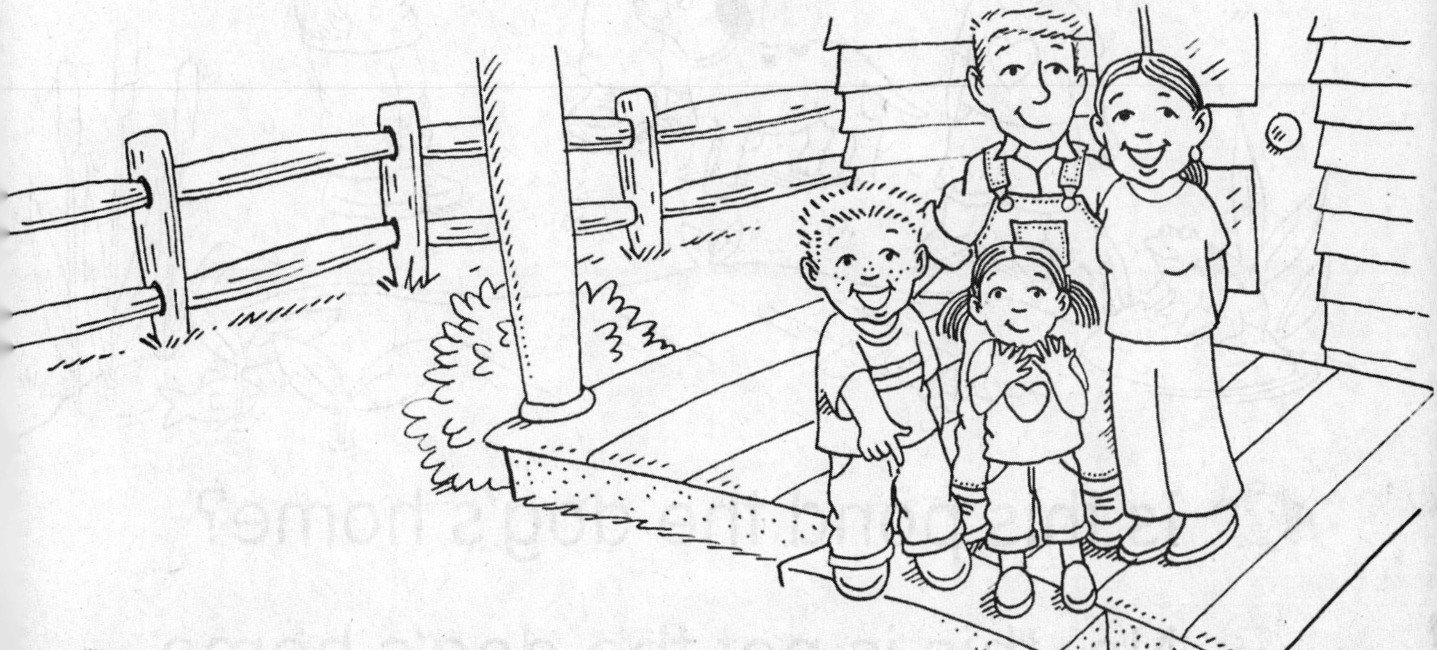

 Look! That dog is lost.

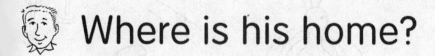

 Let's help him get home.

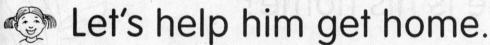

 Where is his home?

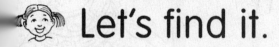

 Let's find it.

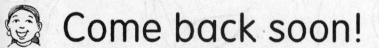

 Come back soon!

Is this pond the dog's home?

No, this is not the dog's home.

Where is his home?

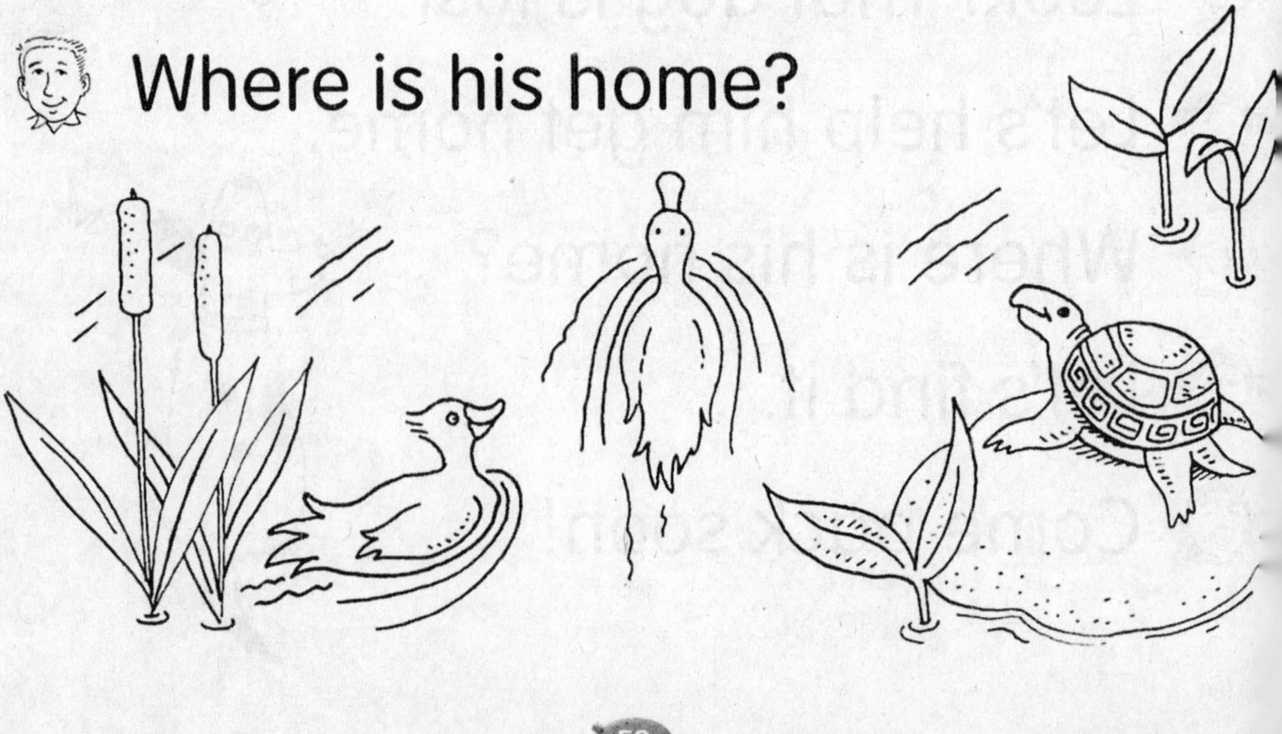

Is this the dog's home?

This is not the dog's home.

Let's go ask Mom now.

Yes! Let's ask Mom now!

 The dog is not lost.

 This is the dog's home.

 Oh! Thank you so much,
Mom and Dad!

Zoom Along

Book 1-2

Name ______________________________

Phonics: Short Vowel /e/e

Lesson 7

▶ **Read the sentences. Circle the sentence that tells about the picture.**

1. Peg fed the dog.
Peg lost the dog.

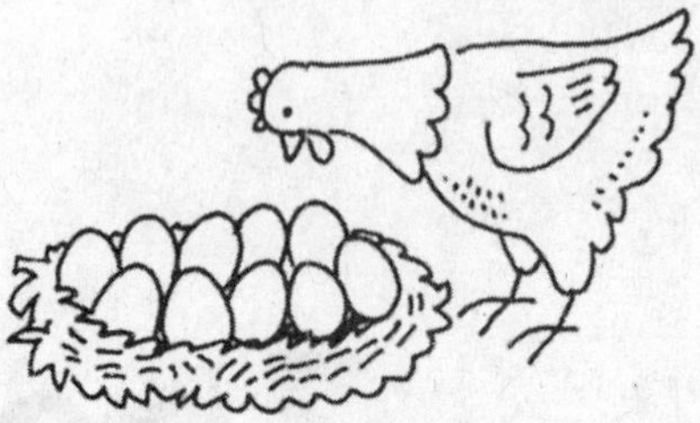

2. This hen has ten pots.
This hen has ten eggs.

3. The pen is on the desk.
The pen is on the dock.

4. That jam is next to go.
That jet is next to go.

5. Jeff is resting.
Jeff is calling.

School-Home Connection

Have your child read aloud all the sentences. Ask your child to tell you the words that have the short e sound, as in *bed*.

Name ______________________

▶ **Read the Spelling Words. Then write each word in the group where it belongs.**

Words with e

______________ ______________

______________ ______________

______________ ______________

______________ ______________

______________ ______________

____

Spelling Words

set
sent
ten
tell
let
get
all
call
make
of

Words without e

____

____

____

____

School-Home Connection

Have your child read each Spelling Word aloud. Talk about how the words are alike and how they are different. Start by comparing the words *set* and *sent*.

Name ______________________________

Circle the word that completes each sentence. Then write the word.

hen **hot**

1. The ______________ can peck.

pot **pet**

2. She has a ______________.

nod **nest**

3. Jess sees a ______________.

end **egg**

4. Ken eats an ______________.

bits **belts**

5. The ______________ will be on them.

School-Home Connection

Have your child read each completed sentence aloud. Ask your child to point to all the words that have the short e sound, as in *bed*.

Name ______________________________

Write a word from the box to complete each sentence.

day	eat	first	said	time	was

1. "You can kick, Tess," he __________.

2. "I will kick __________."

3. It __________ a good kick.

4. Now it's __________ for Tess to kick.

5. It's the best kick of the __________!

School-Home Connection

Point to the word *eat*, and have your child read it. Ask your child to use this word in a sentence.

Name ______________________________

Read about the animals. Complete the sentences. Tell how the animals are the same.

The dog is big.
It is a pet.
It eats fast.

The hen is little.
It is a pet, too.
It pecks to eat.

1. The hen and the dog ______________________.

2. They ______________________  food.

Now complete these sentences. Tell how the animals are different.

3. The dog is ______________. It eats ______________.

4. The hen is ______________. It ______________ to eat.

School-Home Connection

Ask your child to think of other ways the animals are alike and different.

Name ______________________

Write the word that completes each sentence.

1. He is in a ____________ van. **back** **black**

2. She likes ____________. **plants** **pants**

3. Meg ____________ to pack. **plans** **pans**

4. The land is ____________. **fat** **flat**

5. They ____________ for him. **cap** **clap**

School-Home Connection

Have your child read the words and sentences aloud to you. Talk about how the words in each word pair are the same and different.

Name ____________________

▶ **Look at the picture. Write exclamations to go with the picture.**

1. ____________________

2. ____________________

3. ____________________

4. ____________________

School–Home Connection

Ask your child to use the words *help*, *look*, and *good* to write exclamations. Encourage your child to make up a story using these exclamations.

Name ______________________________________

▶ **Circle the sentence that tells about each picture.**

1. The dog gets a bath.
The dog gets a bat.

2. Dad and Mom met Beth.
They met on the path.

3. The dog sits with a cat.
The dog thinks that is a bat.

4. Mr. Glen is tenth.
Mr. Glen is thin.

5. Jill sits with the dolls.
Jill wants the fifth doll.

6. I thank the vet for her help.
The pet thanks the vet.

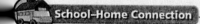

School–Home Connection

Point to the words *bath* and *bat*. Talk about how the words are alike and different.

Name ______________________

▶ **Read the Spelling Words. Then write each word in the group where it belongs.**

Words with th

Words without th

Spelling Words

then
them
this
that
path
with
ten
get
said
was

School-Home Connection

Have your child read each Spelling Word aloud. Then take turns saying the words to each other and writing them.

Name ______________________________

▶ **Look at each picture. Write a word from the box to complete each sentence.**

sixth	thin	path	that	Beth

1. ______________ waters the plants.

2. Ken is ______________ in line.

3. The cat is not too ______________.

4. I like ______________ fish.

5. Dot is on the ______________.

School–Home Connection

Have your child read each completed sentence aloud. Together, think of other words that begin or end with *th*.

Name ______________________

Write a word from the box to complete each sentence.

don't	her	line	Mr.
new	says	water	

1. Meg picks up __________ things.

2. Todd __________ he will help.

3. Cliff will __________ the plants.

4. I __________ want to get wet.

5. Tom gets a __________ cloth.

6. __________ Glenn is glad to help.

School–Home Connection

Have your child read each sentence aloud. Then ask him or her to point to the word *line* in the box and use the word in a sentence.

Name ___________________________

Read about Tim's dog. Write three details that tell about the dog.

Tim has a dog. His dog is called Meg. She is a black dog. She is a little fat. The dog is so soft. Tim is glad he has Meg for a pet.

1. ___________________________

2. ___________________________

3. ___________________________

School–Home Connection
Ask your child to think of a favorite toy or a pet. Have him or her tell details about it.

Name ______________________________

▶ Circle the word that completes each sentence. Then write the word.

snack stack

1. Jed fed his pet a __________.

skill spill

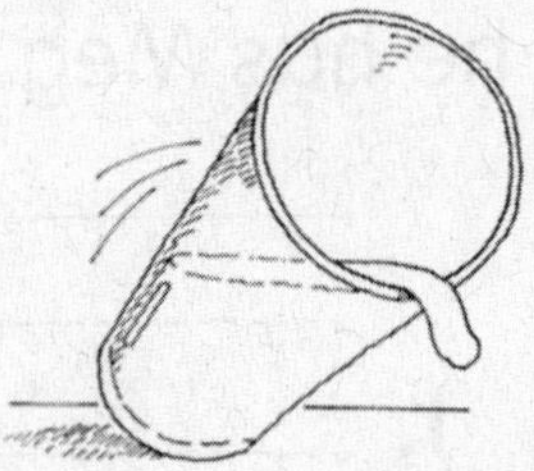

2. The milk will __________.

smells spells

3. The ham __________ good.

slick stick

4. The dog gets the __________.

slim swim

5. Todd and Beth can __________.

School-Home Connection

Talk about the pictures. Say each sentence with the incorrect word. Have your child read the sentence correctly.

Name ____________________

▶ **Look at the picture. Write two sentences to go with the picture. Use nouns that name places and people.**

1. ____________________

2. ____________________

School-Home Connection

Have your child name people and places as you write them down. Then read the list to your child and ask him or her to say a sentence using each name.

Name ________________________________

▶ Write a word from the box to complete each sentence.

jump	but	tuck	fun	dust	must

1. Glen and Russ have ____________ acting like frogs.

2. "First, we ____________ sit like this."

3. "Then we ____________ up and down."

4. They kick up a lot of ____________.

5. Russ can't hop fast, ____________ Glenn can.

School-Home Connection

Ask your child to read aloud the completed sentences. Have him or her point to words that have the short *u* sound, as in *hut*.

Name ______________________

▶ **Read the Spelling Words. Then write each word in the group where it belongs.**

Words with u

______________ ______________

______________ ______________

______________ ______________

______________ ______________

______________ ______________

______________ ______________

Words without u

______________ ______________

______________ ______________

______________ ______________

______________ ______________

Spelling Words

us
bus
must
cut
cub
club
with
then
don't
says

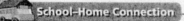

School-Home Connection

Have your child read each Spelling Word aloud. Then have your child identify the words with the short *u* sound.

Name ____________________

Cross out the word that is wrong.
Write the correct word.

1. This pig is in the mad.

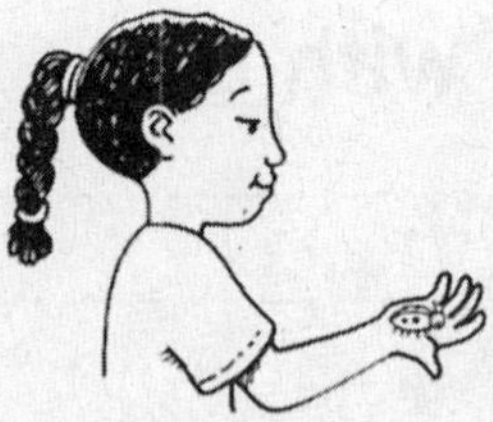

2. A beg is on her hand.

3. A net is good to eat.

4. He fills the jog.

5. She sits on a stamp.

6. The deck swims in the pond.

School-Home Connection

Ask your child to read each sentence with the incorrect word and then reread it with the correct word.

Name ____

▶ **Write a word from the box to complete each sentence.**

be	does	food	grow	live	many

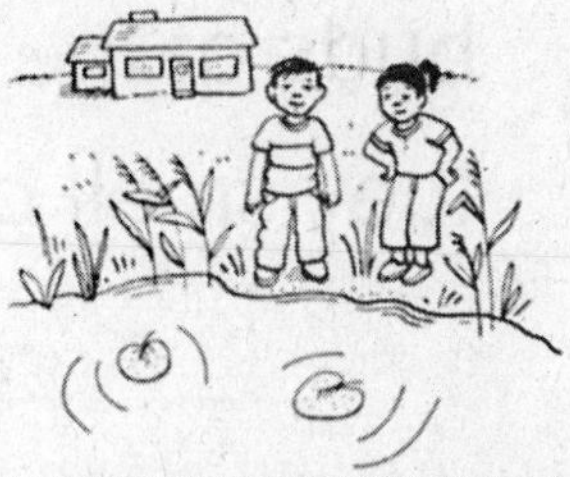

1. They ______________ next to a pond.

2. Plants ______________ tall next to the water.

3. There are ______________ bugs that like the pond.

4. Ducks come there to look for ______________.

5. Beth likes to ______________ at the pond.

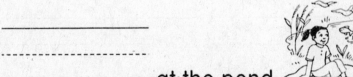

School-Home Connection

Point to each word in the box, and ask your child to use it in a sentence. Help your child write a sentence using the word *does*.

Name ______________________________

▶ Read about the plant. Write three details that tell about this plant.

I have a plant. It is in a black pot. This plant has a tall stem. There are two pink buds at the top. The buds are soft, and they smell good, too.

1. ______________________________

2. ______________________________

3. ______________________________

School-Home Connection

Ask your child to think of a favorite game or toy. Have him or her tell details about it that make it a favorite.

Name ______________________________

▶ Write r as the second letter in each word to make a new word. Then use the new words to complete the sentences.

tuck	+ r	
cab	+ r	
tip	+ r	
fog	+ r	

1. The __________ and the __________ pack some bags.

2. They will go on a __________ in a __________.

School–Home Connection

With your child, think of words that begin with the letters *br*, *dr*, *gr*, and *tr*. Have your child write the first two letters of each word you say.

Name ____________________

▶ **Circle the nouns. Then write four sentences. Use a noun from the box in each sentence.**

dig	dog	fox
hand	has	map
raft	sled	soft

1. ____________________

2. ____________________

3. ____________________

4. ____________________

School-Home Connection

Have your child draw pictures of animals. Help him or her label each picture with the animal's name.

Name ______________________________

▶ **Circle the sentence that tells about each picture.**

1. 

Frank bangs the drums.

Frank bags the drums.

2. 

This man sings a song.

This man is a king.

3. 

Beth rings the bell.

Beth brings the bell.

4. 

The bug hangs on a plant.

The bug flings the plant.

5. 

Brent likes to swim.

Brent likes to swing.

School-Home Connection

Write the words *bag* and *bang*. Have your child read the words aloud. Talk about how each word sounds and how it is spelled.

Name ________________________________

Read the Spelling Words. Then write each word in the group where it belongs.

Words with ng

______________ ______________

______________ ______________

______________ ______________

______________ ______________

______________ ______________

______________ ______________

Words without ng

______________ ______________

______________ ______________

______________ ______________

Spelling Words

long
song
sing
ring
bring
thing
us
must
does
food

School-Home Connection

Write the Spelling Words *long* and *sing*. Have your child change one letter in each word to make other Spelling Words (*song* and *ring*).

Name ____________________

▶ Write a word from the box to complete each sentence.

long	brings	swung	ring	sang	wings

1. Bess has a ______________ on her hand.

2. Frank ______________ at the ball.

3. Some bugs have ______________.

4. This crab has ______________ legs.

5. Mom ______________ me food to eat.

School-Home Connection

Have your child read each completed sentence aloud. Together, think of other words that end with *ng*.

Name ______________________________

▶ **Write a word from the box to complete each sentence.**

arms	every	feet	head
school	use	way	your

1. Frank sings at ______________ with his class.

2. Mr. Ling says, "Look this ______________."

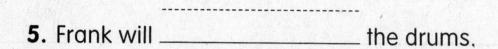

3. Then Mr. Ling says, "Clap ______________ hands."

4. Frank swings his ______________, too.

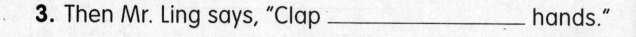

5. Frank will ______________ the drums.

6. Frank taps his ______________.

School-Home Connection

Ask your child to point to the words *every* and *head*. Have him or her use the words to write sentences.

Name ______________________________

Read the story. Finish the sentences.

It was a hot day. Glenn wanted to swim. "Mom, will you go with me so I can swim?" Glenn asked.

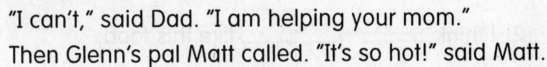

"I can't, Glenn. I am fixing the sink now," said Mom.

Glenn asked his dad, "Will you swim with me?"

"I can't," said Dad. "I am helping your mom."

Then Glenn's pal Matt called. "It's so hot!" said Matt. "Do you want to go with my dad and me to swim?"

"Yes, I do!" said Glenn. "Thank you!"

1. Glenn wanted to ______________________________.

2. First, ______________________ said no. Dad did, too.

3. Glenn went to swim with ______________________________.

School-Home Connection

Have your child read the story aloud. Ask your child why Glenn wanted to swim. (because it was a hot day) Then ask what happened at the end.

Name ______________________

Write the contraction for the two words. Then read the sentence.

We will

1. ______________ get a snack to eat.

you will

2. I think ______________ like this food.

He will

3. ______________ make some ham for us.

she will

4. I think ______________ have water to drink.

I will

5. ______________ have some water, too.

School-Home Connection

Say sentences using the contractions *I'll, they'll,* and *we'll.* Ask your child to say each sentence again, but with the two words that make up each contraction.

Name ______________________

▶ **Look around the room. What do you see? Write sentences that tell how many you see of some things.**

1. ______________________

2. ______________________

3. ______________________

School-Home Connection

Play a game with your child. Name something that you have in your home or family. Have your child say a sentence that tells how many you have.

Name ______________________________

Write the word that completes the sentence.

trunk thorn tore

1. A ____________ cut my leg.

fork flock corn

2. The ____________ fell on the mat.

fort forest frog

3. The frog lives in the ____________.

more well wore

4. Sam ____________ a jacket in the cold.

stop sort store

5. He gets food at the ____________.

School-Home Connection
Have your child read each word and sentence aloud. Talk about how the choices for each item are alike and how they are different.

Name ______________________________

Read the Spelling Words. Then write each word in the group where it belongs.

Words with or

______________ ______________

______________ ______________

______________ ______________

______________ ______________

______________ ______________

Words without or

______________ ______________

______________ ______________

______________ ______________

Spelling Words

or
for
form
more
store
sort
long
bring
your
head

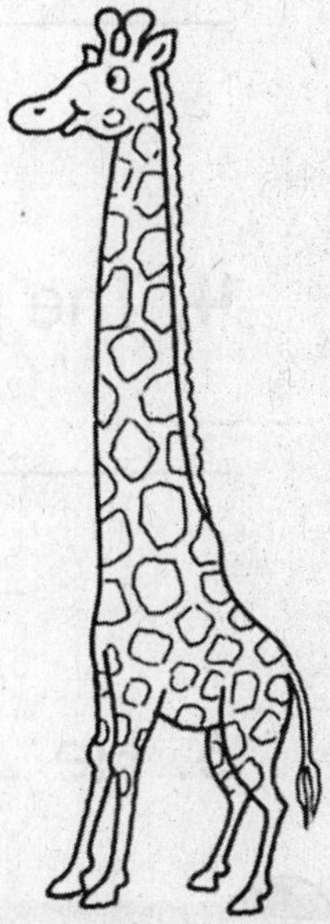

School-Home Connection

Play a version of *I Spy* with your child using the Spelling Word list. Say, for example, "I Spy words with *f*." Have your child write the words.

Name ______________________________

▶ Look at each picture. Write a word from the box to complete each sentence.

more	storm	snores	corn	snorts	shore

1. The pig eats lots of ______________.

2. The pig ______________ as he naps.

3. The ______________ will stop soon.

4. The pig wants ______________ food.

5. He ______________ at us.

School-Home Connection

Have your child read each word in the box aloud. Together, think of other words spelled with *or* or *ore* that have the /ôr/ sound.

Name ______________________________

Write a word from the box to complete each sentence.

animals	cold	fish	from
their	under	very	

1. I have pet ________________.

2. One swims ________________ a big fish.

3. My water is ________________. The water for my fish is not cold.

4. My pals have ________________, too.

5. Doris has a ________________ plump rabbit.

6. The twins run with ________________ dog.

School-Home Connection

Have your child write a sentence using the word *from*. Encourage him or her to use the other words in sentences, too.

Name ______________________

▶ **Look at the pictures and read the sentences. Complete the sentence that follows by telling how the things are alike.**

Helen has socks.
They are on her feet.
Her socks are red.

Helen has mittens, too.
They are on her hands.
They are black.

1. The socks and mittens belong to ______________.

____.

▶ **Now tell how the things are different.**

2. The socks ______________________________.

3. The mittens ______________________________.

School-Home Connection

Together, think of items of clothing that your child wears. Talk about how the items are alike and how they are different.

Name ______________________

▶ **Say each word and picture name together to make a new word. Write the new word. Then use the words to complete the sentences.**

 + hill =	______
sand + 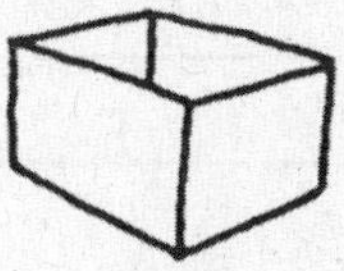 =	______
 + pack =	______

1. Grant went to dig in the ______________.

2. An ______________ was hidden in the grass.

3. Ants got into his ______________.

School-Home Connection

Have your child read the words and sentences aloud. Together, think of other words that can be put together to make new words.

Name ______________________________

▶ **Write a letter to a friend. Tell about yourself and your family. Write special names and titles correctly.**

____

Dear ______________________________,

Your pal,

School-Home Connection

Write a list with your child of special names and titles of people you know. Read them together. Point out the capital letters.

Name ______________________

▶ Write the word that completes the sentence.

1. I made eggs. They are on a ____________.

dish **dash**

2. I can make ____________, too.

fish **short**

3. I ____________ I could make apple crisp.

shrug **wish**

4. I will ____________ for apples.

ship **shop**

5. I will get a ____________, too.

radish **finish**

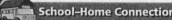

School-Home Connection

Have your child read each completed sentence aloud. Ask your child what is the same about all the word choices. (They all have the *sh* sound.)

Name ______________________________

▶ **Read the Spelling Words. Then write each word in the group where it belongs.**

Words with sh

______ ______

______ ______

______ ______

______ ______

______ ______

Words without sh

______ ______

______ ______

______ ______

______ ______

Spelling Words

- shop
- shot
- shut
- rush
- wish
- fish
- for
- more
- from
- very

School-Home Connection

Ask your child to write all the Spelling Words with *o* on a sheet of paper. Encourage your child to continue this activity with *u*, *i*, and *e*.

Name ______________________

Phonics: Digraph
/sh/*sh*

Lesson 12

▶ **Write the word from the box that completes the sentence.**

cash	finished	shop
shelf	rush	

1. We will ______________ at the mall.

2. I have ______________ to get a doll.

3. I see dolls on a ______________.

4. I ______________ to get a doll.

5. We have ______________.

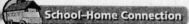

School-Home Connection

Have your child read each completed sentence aloud. Together, think of other words with the *sh* sound, as in *shop* and *rush*.

Name ____________________

▶ Write a word from the box to complete the sentence.

happy	came	could	gold
made	night	saw	were

1. The king gave Doris a ____________ ring.

2. The gift made her very ____________.

3. Frog ____________ to look at her ring.

4. He asked if he ____________ hold it.

5. The ring was ____________ just for Doris.

School-Home Connection

Ask your child to read aloud the words in the box and the completed sentences. Then invite your child to create sentences to continue the story, using *night, saw,* and *were.*

Name ______________________________________

▶ Read each story beginning. Circle the picture that shows the setting.

1. This morning, I helped Mom pick corn.
"That bucket is filled with corn now," Mom said.
"Let's go get some eggs from the hens."
"Then can we go to see the pigs?" I asked.
"Yes, we will go to see the pigs, too," Mom said.

2. It was time for bed.
"Is there a blanket I can have?" Ellen asked Bess.
"My blanket is not soft."
"I will give you my blanket," Bess said. "Will you let me go on the top bunk?"

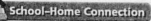

School-Home Connection

Talk about a story that you and your child know. Ask your child to tell you where and when the story takes place.

Name ____________________________________

▶ Write the words where they belong in the puzzle.

crab	skunk	blanket	sled	block

1. 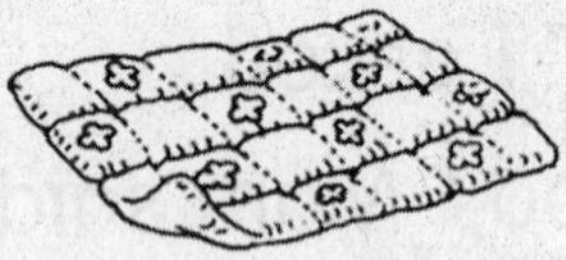

2. 

3. 

4. 

5. 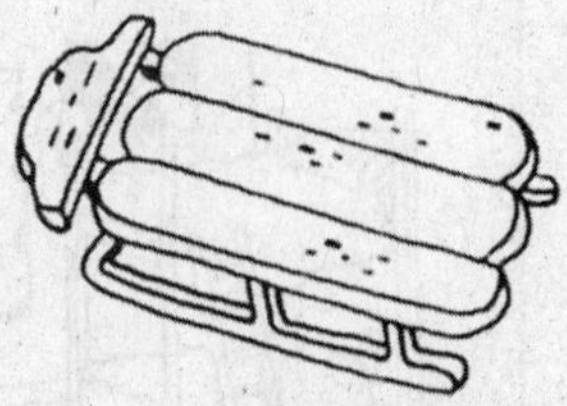

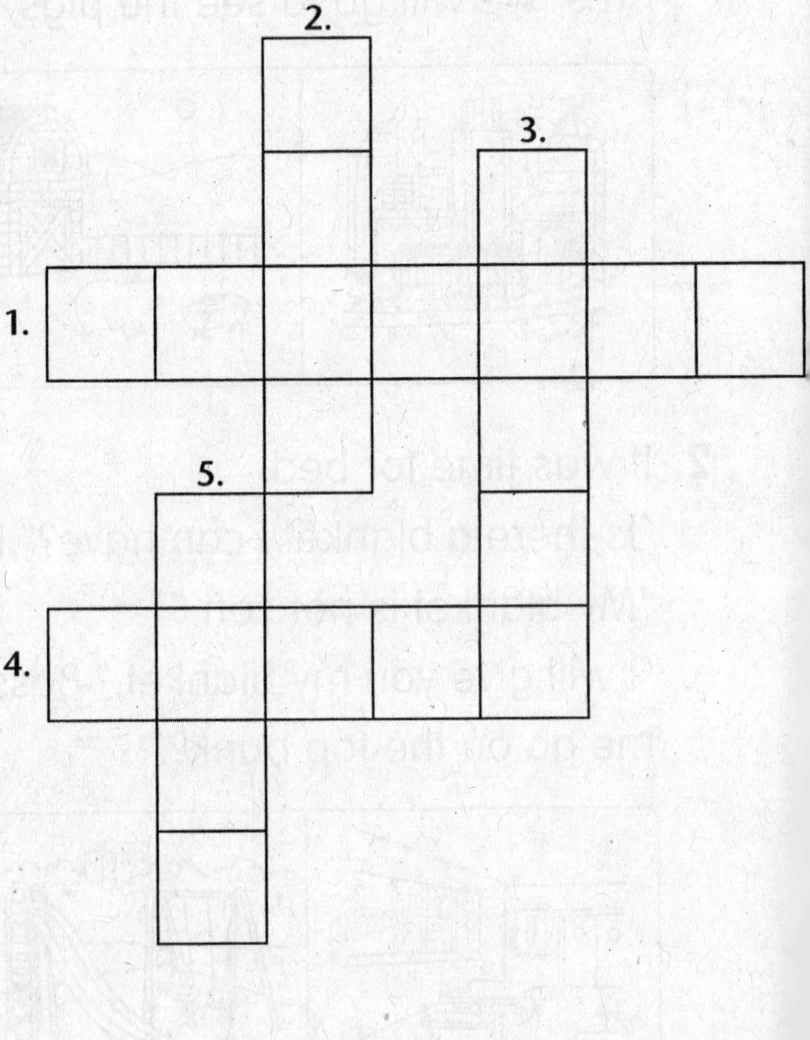

School-Home Connection

Write the words *snack*, *brush*, and *flip*. Say a clue for each, not in order, and have your child point to the correct word.

Name ______________________________

▶ **Circle each sentence that is written correctly.**

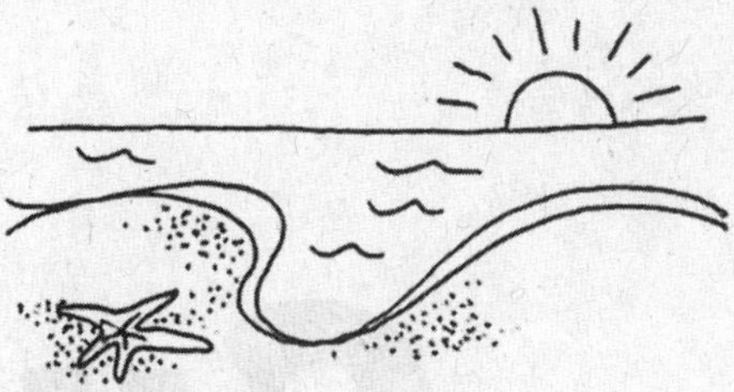

1. Hank lives on York Way.
2. Beth lives by flag cliff.
3. Trish lives next to the Red Mitten Store.
4. Todd lives by sunset shore.
5. Dennis and Jen live on top of Rust Hill.

▶ **Now write the other sentences correctly.**

6. ______________________________

____

7. ______________________________

____

School-Home Connection
With your child, draw a map of your neighborhood. Write the names of special places such as stores, schools, and churches. Use capital letters.

Cut-Out/ Fold-Up Books

Meg's Bad Day

1

"Yes, I have time, Meg" said Ted. 3

"Ted!" said Meg.

6 "Help me fix the well!"

8 "You fixed my bad day!" said Meg.

Fold

Fold

"Ted!" called Meg. "Will you fix the bed? A leg fell off."

2

Fold

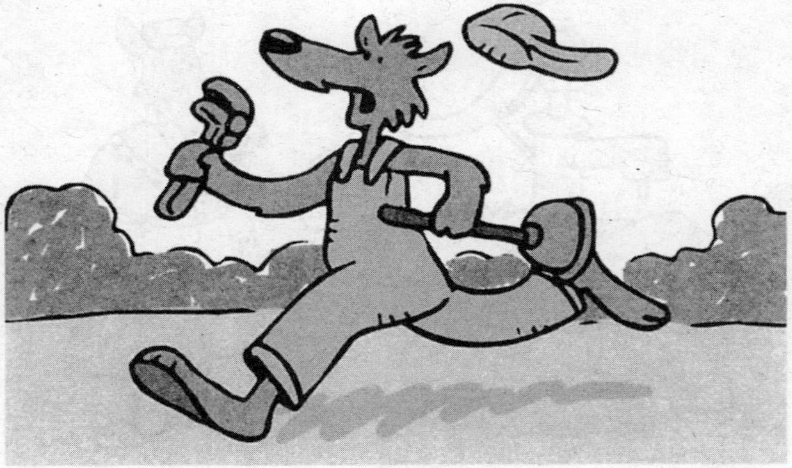

"Here I come, Meg!" said Ted.

7

"Ted," said Meg. "All day we see this mess. Can you fix it?"

4

Fold

"You bet!" Ted said to Meg.

5

Where Is Seth?

1

Is he at home? 3

6 "I don't see Seth," Mom says.

8 "Here I am, Mom!" says Seth.

Fold

Fold

2 Mom looks for Seth.

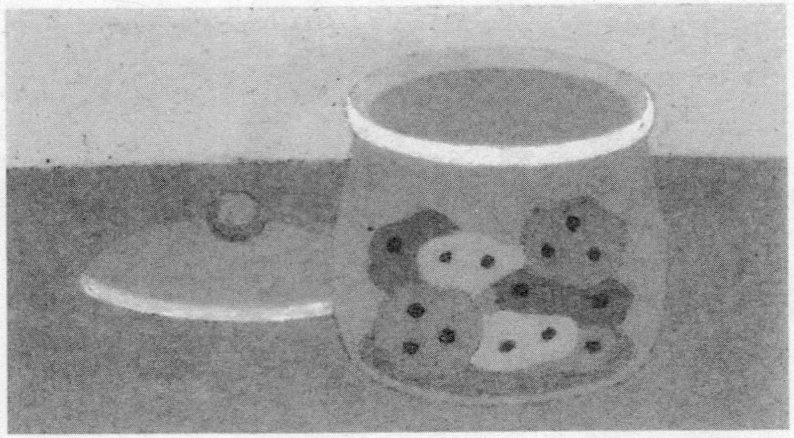

Did Seth eat here?
Mom thinks so. 7

Fold

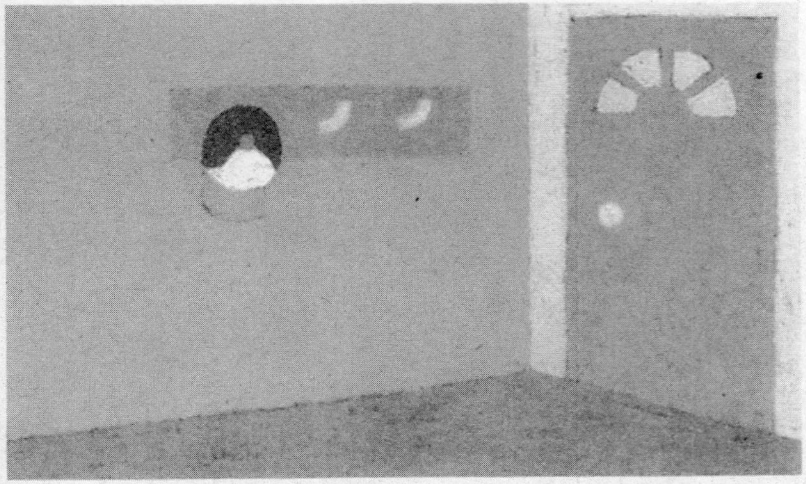

4 He left his new cap on a peg.

He set his bag down here. 5

Fold

We Can Find It

1

"I see many things up here,"
says Scott. "Here is the pig."

3

"Where can my cat be?" says Scott.
"We can all hunt for it," says Tim.

6

"Thanks! Now we all
have what we want."

8

Fold

Fold

"Where can my pig be?" asks Bess.

2 "Scott, do you see my pig?"

"What does it look like?" Tim asks.

"I see the cat, Scott," says Bess. 7

Fold

"I want my food," says Tim.

4 "Where can my food be?"

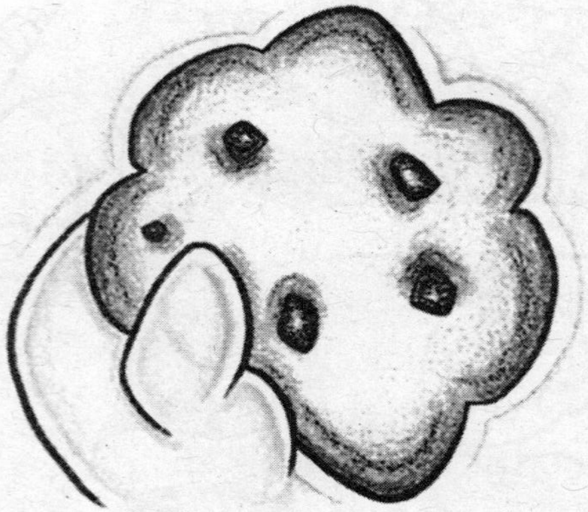

"I will get it for you," says Scott.

He gives the food to Tim. 5

Fold

8 Now it is time to go back home.

Frog Songs

1

6 This is the way they like to sing.

Fred uses his arms and feet to hop.
He has lots of bugs to eat. 3

Fold

Fold

Fred is a frog at Moss Pond.
He likes to hop on every rock.

2

This is the way Fred uses his arms.
The song ends with a bang!

7

Fold

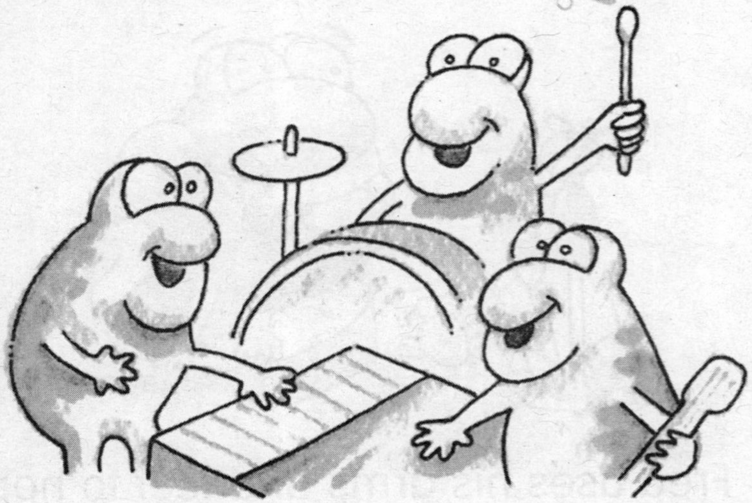

Fred sings songs at school.

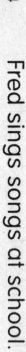

4

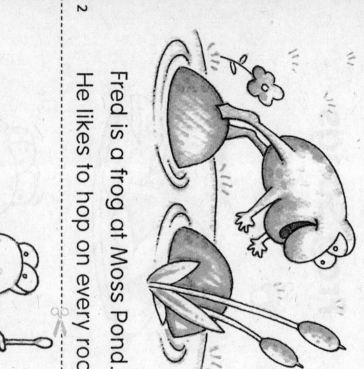

Every day they make up songs.

5

Fold

8 I like kisses from Mom very much!

One More Thing

1

Fold

"This is the last one.

6 Then you'll go to bed.

"Mom, can I have just one more?" 3

Fold

This snack is from Mom.
I like this snack very much.

2

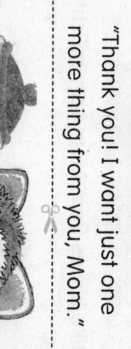

"Thank you! I want just one
more thing from you, Mom."

7

Fold

"Here's one more for you.
Then it will be time for bed."

4

"I see one more, Mom.
Can I have one more from here?"

5

Brad Shops for Fish

1

They picked out a fish tank. They
got many things for their fish.

3

Dad got fish food from the shelf.
Brad looked at the fish. He saw
some that were gold and black.

6

Brad made a home for his fish.
How many fish do you see?

8

Fold

Fold

Brad and his dad came to the fish shop.

2

Brad picked his fish. They were two very big fish. Now he and his dad could go home.

7

Fold

Some rocks, shells, and a ship could look grand.

4

They got plants to make their fish happy.

5

Fold

The Frog and the Ox

Characters

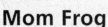

Mom Frog | Dad Frog | Granddad | Jack | Jill

Ribbit, ribbit. Ribbit, ribbit.

It's a hot day at the pond!

Yes! I am happy I am in the cold water.

Here come some animals looking for a drink.

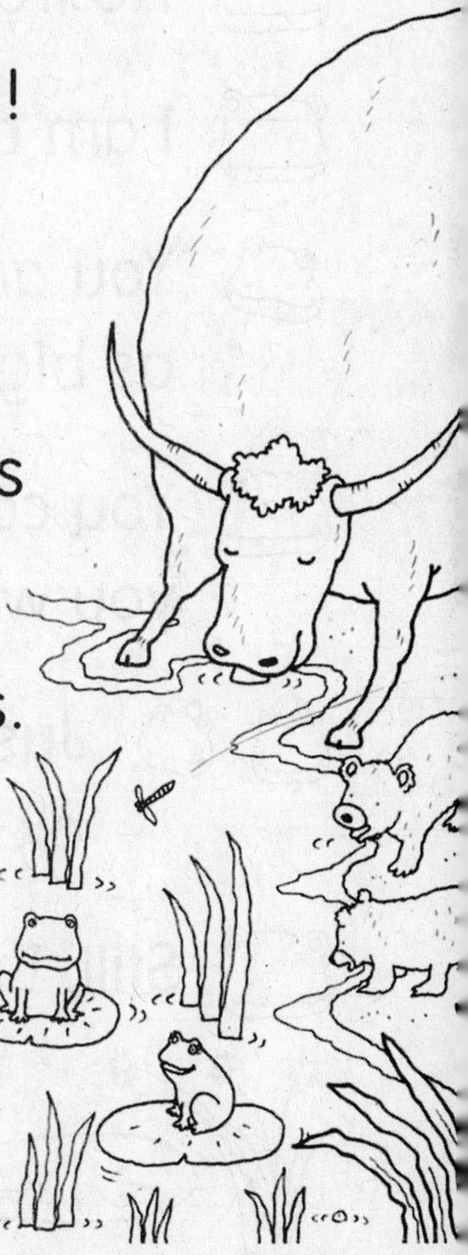

I see an ox and two cubs.

That ox is very big.

Very, very big!

I wish I were that big.

No frog could be that big.

I am a very big frog.

You *are* big, but frogs don't get as big as an ox.

You could not live like a frog if you were that big.

Just think of the splash if an ox jumped into the water!

Still, I wish I were that big.

What are you doing?

He has puffed himself
up to make himself look big.

Mom says, "If you want to grow,
you must eat a lot of bugs."

He is still puffed up.

Stop now! You are still
smaller than the ox.

You must use your head.
You can't be as big as an ox.

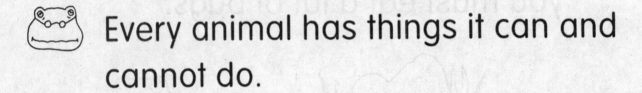

That makes me so mad! Why can't I grow as big as I want?

Every animal has things it can and cannot do.

Don't forget that an ox can't jump like we can.

Then I like being a small frog.

Me, too!

Ribbit, ribbit. Ribbit, ribbit.

Reach for the Stars

Book 1-3

Name ______________________________

▶ Circle the word that completes each sentence. Then write the word.

branch **brush** **brand**

1. The cat sits on a ____________.

chunk **crush** **crutch**

2. Chad must use a ____________.

best **bent** **bench**

3. We sit on the ____________ to eat.

catch **chest** **chunk**

4. My doll is in the ____________.

desk **ditch** **dish**

5. The dog is in the ____________.

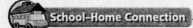

School-Home Connection

Have your child read the sentences aloud. Together, think of more words with *ch* or *tch*.

Name ________________________

Read the Spelling Words. Then write each word in the group where it belongs.

Words with <u>ch</u>

Words without <u>ch</u>

Spelling Words

- chip
- chin
- inch
- such
- catch
- match
- wish
- shop
- saw
- were

School-Home Connection

Have your child read each Spelling Word aloud. Ask him or her to circle the two Spelling Words that have a *t*. *(catch, match)*

Name ____

▶ Circle the sentence that tells about each picture.

1. Mitch is the chess champ.

   Mitch chomps his lunch.

2. Rich will sketch the branch.

   Rich will fetch the stick.

3. Some chicks will hatch soon.

   The children check the test.

4. Chad does not like punch.

   Chad does not like to pitch.

5. Ellen can stitch a patch.

   Ellen can sketch an ostrich.

School-Home Connection

Have your child read each sentence aloud. Ask him or her to draw a picture for a sentence that is not circled.

Name ______________________

Write a word from the box to complete each sentence.

air	fly	friends	grew
need	play	rain	watch

1. I see a robin ______________ in the air.

2. My ______________ see it, too.

3. Does it want to ______________ with us?

4. We ______________ the robin make a nest.

5. The robin will ______________ to rest.

School-Home Connection

Write each word from the box on a separate slip of paper. Place the words face down. Have your child pick a word, read it aloud, and then use it in a sentence.

Name ______________________________

Think about what happens in each picture. Then answer each question.

1. What happens to the plant first?

2. What does the plant get next?

3. What happens last?

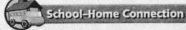

School-Home Connection

Together, talk about how animals and plants grow. Talk about the order in which the events happen.

Name ____________________

Phonics:
Inflection *-es*

Lesson 13

▶ **Add es to the words in the box. Then write the correct word in each sentence.**

toss	sketch	branch	buzz	fix	dish

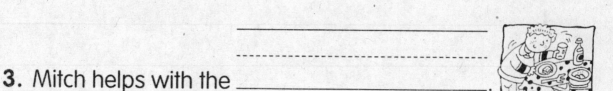

1. Mr. Sanchez ____________ my backpack.

2. Liz ____________ the ball.

3. Mitch helps with the ____________.

4. Meg ____________ a finch.

5. A storm made ____________ fall.

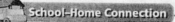

School–Home Connection

Write the words *mash, blush, glass,* and *itch*. Ask your child to make new words by adding -*es*. Have your child draw a picture for each word he or she makes.

Name ____________________

▶ **Write sentences about your favorite two months. Tell what you like to do during each month. Write the sentences correctly.**

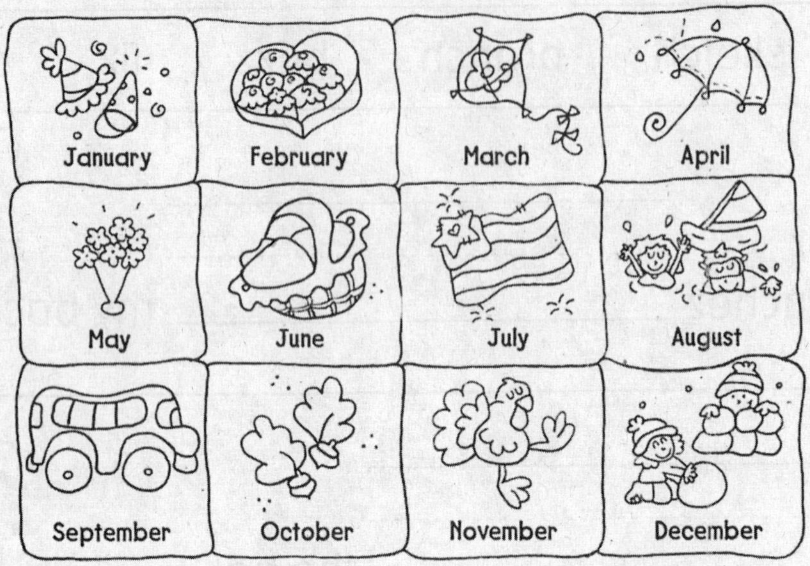

1. ____________________

2. ____________________

School-Home Connection

Ask your child what the names of the months all have in common when you write them. (They all start with a capital letter.) Talk about what you like best about different months.

Name ____________________

Circle the word that completes each sentence. Then write the word.

from farm form

____

1. We go to visit a ____________.

chat cart chart

____

2. There is an animal ____________ on a wall.

band barn born

____

3. Some animals are in the ____________.

hard had here

____

4. Some of us help with ____________ chores.

starch stork start

____

5. We ____________ to get in the bus to go home.

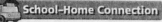

School-Home Connection

Have your child read each completed sentence aloud and explain why he or she chose each word.

Name ______________________________

▶ **Read the Spelling Words. Then write each word in the group where it belongs.**

Words with ar

Words without ar

Spelling Words

- far
- farm
- arm
- art
- part
- park
- chin
- such
- fly
- watch

School-Home Connection

Have your child read each Spelling Word aloud. Write the word *art* and have your child add one letter to make the word *part*. Repeat with *arm* and *farm*.

Name ______________________________

▶ Cross out the word that is wrong.
Write the correct word.

1. We are at a form.

____

2. We went into the born.

____

3. Mr. Brent got a cord.

____

4. We went to the pork.

____

5. I have a cast on my am.

____

6. Dad will use the cat to shop.

____

School-Home Connection

Say a sentence with one incorrect word. Ask your child to say the sentence correctly.

Name ______________________

▶ **Write the word from the box that completes the sentence.**

again	feel	house	know
loud	Mrs.	put	say

1. ____________ Marsh asked Scarlet to help.

2. Scarlet and the dog went out of the ____________.

3. Scarlet was happy to play with the dog ____________.

4. "I ____________ he wants to run in the yard," Scarlet said.

5. The dog had a ____________ bark.

School-Home Connection

Have your child find the words *feel*, *say*, and *put* in the box. Ask him or her to use them in sentences.

Name ____________________

Circle the picture that shows who is telling each story. Then circle the sentence that tells why the author wrote it.

Helping Lost Pets by Liz Smith

My dog, Max, has a tag. The tag tells where his home is. It tells who to call if Max is lost. If you find a lost pet, look at its tag.

1.  

2. Liz Smith wants us to know how to help lost pets.

Liz Smith wants us to get a dog.

Dog Fun! by Martin Hill

Bark! Sniff! Run and jump! Lick! Wag! Thump, thump, thump! Let's go to the park! Let's have fun! I'll catch the ball. I'll run and run!

3.   

4. The author wants us to have fun reading this.

The author wants us to pet a dog.

School-Home Connection

Talk about a story that you and your child know. Discuss why the author might have written the story.

Name ______________________________

Write a word from the box to complete each sentence.

banged	started	checks
looked	acting	thinks

1. Tom was ______________ in the play.

2. He ______________ to say his part.

3. Helen ______________ the drums.

4. Mrs. Hill ______________ the clock.

5. She ______________ we will finish the play soon.

School-Home Connection

Have your child read each completed sentence aloud. Together, practice adding *-s*, *-ed*, and *-ing* to other words and using the new words in sentences.

Name ________________________

Write three sentences about your favorite holidays. Write the names of the holidays correctly.

1. ________________________

2. ________________________

3. ________________________

School–Home Connection

Make a list of holidays that your family celebrates. Talk about each holiday. Encourage your child to draw and label a picture for his or her favorite holiday.

Name ________________________________

▶ Read the sentences. Circle the sentence that tells about the picture.

1. 

Cliff has a quilt on his bed.

Cliff has a quack on his bed.

2. 

"I will quit pecking corn."

"When will my eggs hatch?"

3. 

"Is this is a quick car?"

"Which ball do you want?"

4. 

The ducks quack all day.

The ducks quit all day.

5. 

Ted quacks at the ball.

Ted whacks the ball.

School-Home Connection

Point to the words *quack* and *whacks*. Talk about how the words are alike and different.

Name ______________________________

▶ **Read the Spelling Words. Then write each word in the group where it belongs.**

Words with wh

______________ ______________

______________ ______________

____

Words with qu

______________ ______________

______________ ______________

____

Other Words

______________ ______________

______________ ______________

Spelling Words

quit
quick
quiz
whiz
which
when
arm
part
house
put

School–Home Connection

Ask your child to point to each Spelling Word with an *i* and read it aloud. Then have him or her read the other words aloud and name the vowels used.

Name ______________________________

Look at each picture. Write the word in the box that completes the sentence.

Which	quick	quit	When	whip	Quinn

1. Karl is so ______________!

2. ______________ has a shell.

3. ______________ can I go out?

4. ______________ one is my gift?

5. He ______________ singing.

School-Home Connection

Have your child read each completed sentence aloud. Together, think of other words that begin with *qu* and *wh*.

Name ______________________________

Write a word from the box to complete each sentence.

about	books	family	name
people	read	work	writing

1. Mark is ______________ a list.

2. The ______________ are on his desk.

3. Beth sits on the rug to ______________.

4. Scarlet tells us ______________ her pet.

5. Marvin prints his ______________.

6. Chuck can ______________ with Tess.

School-Home Connection

Have your child read *people* and *family*. Ask your child to name the people in your family.

Name ____

Read each group of sentences. Write 1, 2, 3, or 4 in front of each sentence to tell the order in which the events happen.

1. ____ A chick comes out of the egg.

____ The egg hatches.

____ The chick grows up to be a hen.

____ A hen sits on her egg.

2. ____ The corn plants grow tall.

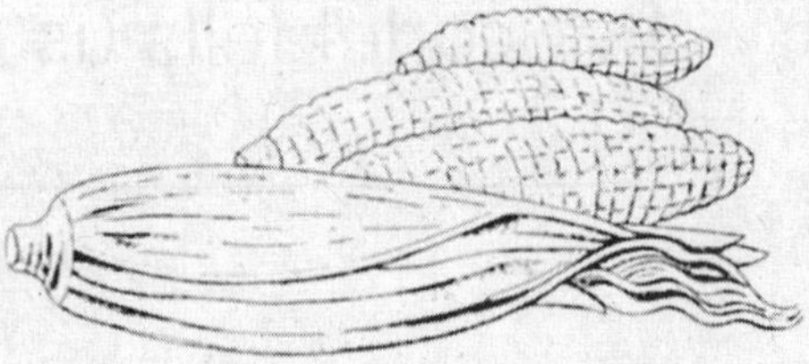

____ It is time to sell the corn.

____ The corn is picked and put in buckets.

____ Corn is planted on a farm.

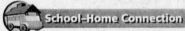

School-Home Connection

Talk about a favorite dish you and your child like to cook. Have your child tell the order in which steps are done to prepare the dish.

Name ___________________________

Write the word that completes the sentence.

1. I ______________ with Janet.

   skipped
   skipping

2. They ______________ the song.

   hummed
   humming

3. She is ______________ to sing.

   planned
   planning

4. He ______________ about his big dog.

   bragged
   bragging

5. Frank's bag ______________.

   ripped
   ripping

School-Home Connection

Ask your child to write the word *skipped* and then underline *skip*. Repeat for other words on this page that end with *ed* or *ing*.

Name ________________________________

▶ Complete the sentence, using <u>I</u> or <u>me</u>.
Write the sentence correctly.

1. ____ like to swim

2. my chicks swim with ____

3. ____ can quack

4. you can see ____

5. ____ am a duck.

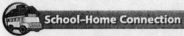

School-Home Connection

Have your child write sentences about an animal that might live in a zoo. Ask him or her to write one sentence using *I* and one sentence using *me*.

Name ____

Circle the sentence that tells about the picture.

1. Her cat is on her shirt.
   The girl pets her cat's soft fur.

2. It turns in her lap and purrs.
   Her pet slurps the water.

3. She will read to her mom.
   She will read to herself.

4. A bird sits and chirps.
   This bird is not on a branch.

5. The girl sees the bird first.
   The bird makes its first nest.

6. The cat and bird are in the dirt.
   The bird flaps as the cat squirms.

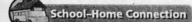

School-Home Connection

Point to the words *girl*, *her*, and *fur* in the second sentence. Have your child read the words aloud. Ask how the words are alike.

Name ______________________

▶ **Read the Spelling Words. Then write each word in the group where it belongs.**

Words with r

______________ ______________

______________ ______________

______________ ______________

______________ ______________

______________ ______________

____

Spelling Words

her
fur
turn
bird
girl
first
quit
when
name
work

Words without r

______________ ______________

____

School-Home Connection

Have your child put a checkmark by the Spelling Words with *ur* and a star by the Spelling Words with *ir*. Then have him or her circle the Spelling Word with *er*.

Name ______________________________

Write a word from the box to complete each sentence.

fur	perched	turn
first	curl	dirt

1. He's the __________ to get into the raft.

2. Now it is Mom and Dad's __________.

3. A bird is __________ in a tree.

4. This animal's __________ is wet.

5. We see it digging in the __________.

School-Home Connection

Write the words *her, thirst,* and *sunburn.* Ask your child to read the words and use them in sentences.

Name ______________________

Write a word from the box to complete each sentence.

always	by	Cow's	join
Please	nice	room	

1. Bird ____________ likes to visit his friends.

2. "Have a ____________ time!" his mom said.

3. Bird went to ____________ barn.

4. "____________ come in," his friend said.

5. "You can ____________ the fun," Hen said.

School-Home Connection

Ask your child to find the words *room* and *by* in the box. Then have him or her write the words in sentences to add to the story above.

Name ______________________________

Read the story. Look at the picture. Circle the sentence that tells the main idea of the story.

1. Hen went on a picnic with her friends. They had sandwiches to eat. Duck and Skunk played catch with a ball. Then they all had fun swimming in the pond.

Animals have fun at a picnic.
The animals swim.

---

2. Summer is here! The sun is up. It is a hot day. Birds are singing. Children are in the park. Some are running. Summer is fun!

It is a hot day.
We have fun in the summer.

---

3. Dan bumped his leg. Now his leg hurts. Dan can see a red spot on his leg. It's starting to swell. He gets help from his mom.

Dan has hurt his leg.
Dan's mom is nice.

School-Home Connection
Read each story with your child. Together, think of a good title for each one. Choose a title that tells what the story is mainly about.

Name ____________________

Look at the picture. Then write the word that completes the sentence.

1. The cat is ____________ than the pig.

smaller
smallest

2. The ostrich is the ____________.

taller
tallest

3. The hen is the ____________.

shorter
shortest

4. The dog's legs are ____________ than the hen's legs.

longer
longest

Try This

Add er and est to the word fast. Draw pictures of three animals. Use the words to label the pictures.

School-Home Connection

Have your child compare things in your home, using words that end in *er* and *est*.

Name ______________________________

Circle each sentence pair that is written correctly.

1. Karl is at the pond. He sits on a bench.

2. Mark and Tom play. He are friends.

3. Beth fixes popcorn. He drinks milk, too.

4. There is a nest. It is on a branch.

Now write the other sentences. Write the pronouns correctly.

5. ______________________________

6. ______________________________

School-Home Connection

Say a sentence, using the name of a person, animal, or thing. Have your child repeat the sentence, using a pronoun in place of the name.

Name ______________________

Circle the word that completes each sentence. Then write the word.

candle little ripple

1. I have a ______________ sister.

purple tickle tattle

2. Mom lets me ______________ her feet.

kettle gobble giggle

3. It makes my sister ______________.

rattle riddle gurgle

4. She likes to play with a ______________.

bubble fiddle bottle

5. She drinks from a ______________.

School-Home Connection

Have your child read each completed sentence aloud. Ask him or her to choose a word that was not circled and to write a sentence with it.

Name ______________________

▶ **Read the Spelling Words. Then write each word in the group where it belongs.**

Spelling Words

hand
handle
wig
wiggle
single
little
turn
girl
by
room

Words with le

______________ ______________

______________ ______________

______________ ______________

Words without le

______________ ______________

______________ ______________

______________ ______________

______________ ______________

School–Home Connection

Write the words *hand, sing, wig,* and *lit.* Have your child read the words aloud. Then ask him or her to add letters to these words to make Spelling Words.

Name ______________________________

Write a word from the box to complete each sentence.

giggle	puddle	ripples
ankles	middle	pebble

1. Jan saw a ________________ of water.

2. She tossed a ________________ into it.

3. It landed in the ________________ of the puddle.

4. It made ________________ in the water.

5. Jan got her ________________ wet.

School-Home Connection

Have your child read each completed sentence aloud. Together, think of other words that end with *le*.

Name ________________________________

▶ **Write a word from the box to complete each sentence.**

buy	carry	money	other
paint	paper	would	

1. Pam has ________ to get what she needs.

2. She'll ________ brushes for her art.

3. She'll need blank ________, too.

4. Mom helps Pam ________ the bags.

5. Pam plans to ________ farm animals.

School-Home Connection

Have your child find the words *other* and *would* in the box. Ask your child to name *other* things he or she *would* like to paint.

Name ______________________________

▶ **Read the sentences. Then circle the best answer to the question.**

Turtles have hard shells. If you startle a turtle, it will go inside its shell. A pond turtle has flat feet. Its feet help it to dig in mud. Other turtles have flippers for swimming.

1. What is this about?

It is about shells.

It is about feet.

It is about turtles.

Many animals hatch from eggs. Birds and ducks hatch from eggs. Their eggs are kept in nests. Turtles hatch from eggs, too. Turtles dig pits in the sand. That's where their eggs are kept. Some insects and frogs hatch from eggs in water.

2. What is this about?

It is about birds.

It is about animals that hatch from eggs.

It is about animals that swim in the water.

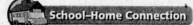

School-Home Connection

Have your child read each story. Ask your child what details helped him or her to figure out the main idea of the story.

Name ______________________________

Add the endings ed and ing to each word. Remember to double the last letter.

	ed	ing
1. jog	jogged	
2. nap		
3. zip		

Write a word from the chart to complete each sentence.

4. Pig ____________ to the camp.

5. Has he ____________ up the tent?

6. Now he is ____________.

School-Home Connection

Write *drip*. Ask your child to rewrite the word with the endings *-ed* and *-ing*. Remind him or her to double the last letter in *drip*.

Name ____________________

▶ **Circle each sentence that is written correctly.**

1. Tom buckles its belt

2. Ella pets her turtle.

3. Ben and Mom pack their bags.

4. The bobcat licks yours fur.

5. Is this magnet yours?

▶ **Now write the other sentences correctly.**

6. ____________________

7. ____________________

School-Home Connection

Find objects in the house that belong to you, your child, and other family members. Talk about the objects using possessive pronouns such as *my, your, our, his, her*.

Name ____________________

▶ Write the words where they belong in the puzzle.

coat	crow	road	snow	soap	throw

1. 
2. 
3. 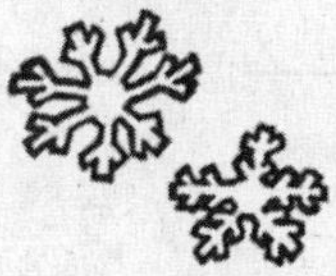
4. 
5. 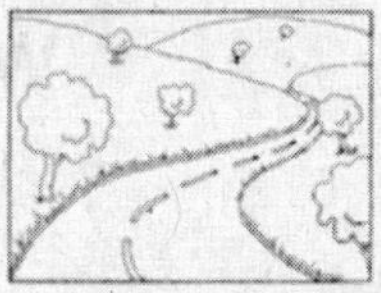
6. 

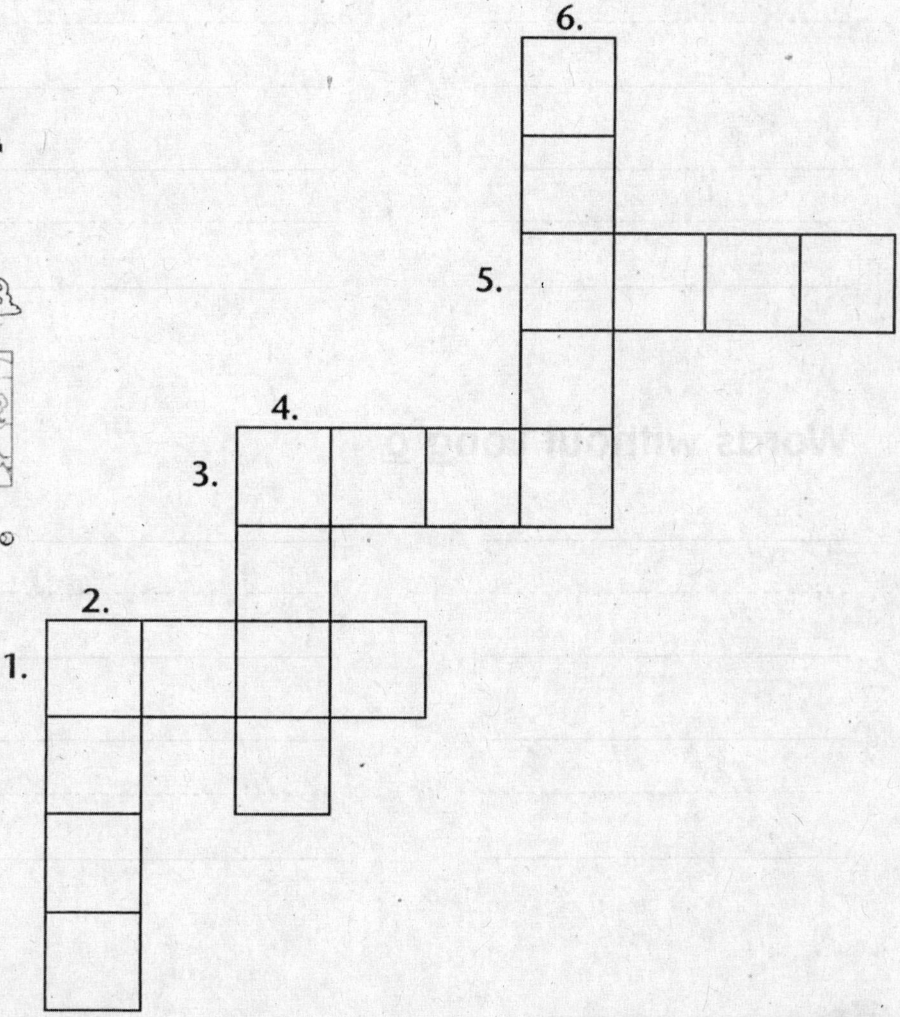

School-Home Connection

Write the words *flow*, *float*, and *follow*. Say a clue for each word, and have your child point to and read the word that matches your clue.

Name ______________________

▶ **Read the Spelling Words. Then write each word in the group where it belongs.**

Spelling Words

- low
- slow
- grow
- road
- soap
- boat
- little
- handle
- carry
- would

Words with Long o

________________ ________________

________________ ________________

________________ ________________

________________ ________________

Words without Long o

________________ ________________

________________ ________________

________________ ________________

School-Home Connection

Write, "I rode to the end of the road and then rowed across the river." Read the sentence aloud and have your child circle the Spelling Word. *(road)*

Name ______________________________

Circle the sentence that tells about each picture.

1. Joan will row the boat.
   Joan will go across the road.

____

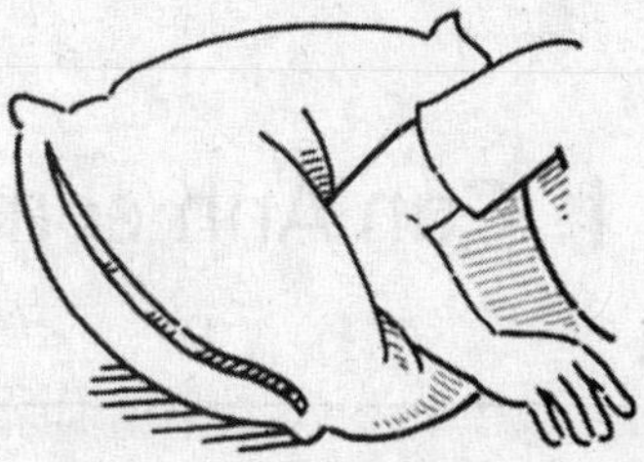

2. There's a fellow by the window.
   He rests his elbow on a pillow.

____

3. The crow follows the goat.
   The toad croaks at a minnow.

____

4. He has a boat on the coast.
   I wore my coat in the snow.

____

5. I soap up as I soak in the tub.
   I have a bath in a tugboat.

____

6. Quinn towed a boat on the pond.
   Quinn floated on the pond.

School-Home Connection

Have your child read each sentence aloud. Ask him or her to choose a sentence that is not circled and draw a picture for it.

Name ________________________________

▶ **Write a word from the box to complete each sentence.**

mouse	our	over
pretty	surprise	three

1. Can Ann come ________ to play?

2. Yes, Ann can come to ________ house.

3. Ann thinks my dolls are ________.

4. I have ________ dolls on my bed.

5. I have a stuffed ________, too.

School-Home Connection

Ask your child to read aloud the word *surprise* from the box. Ask your child to describe a surprise that he or she has enjoyed.

Name ______________________________

Read each story. Then circle the sentence that tells why the author wrote the story.

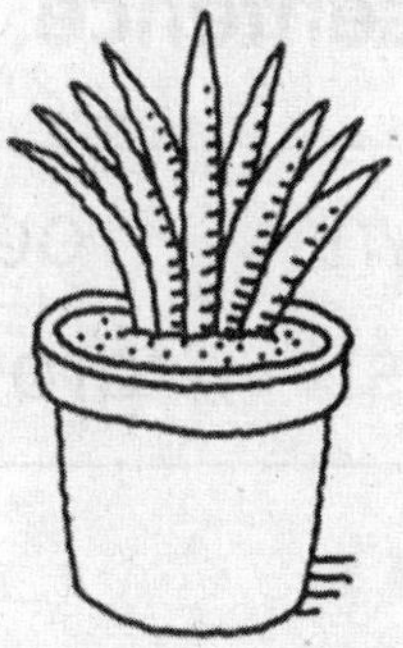

Plants

by Brent Hall

All plants need water to live. Some plants need only a little water. Other plants need a lot. Plants need sun, too. Most potted plants are kept next to a window.

1. Brent Hall wants us to know about water.

Brent Hall wants us to know what plants need.

Helen's Dog

by Fran Miller

Helen was watering her plants. She spilled some water. There was a puddle at her feet. She didn't have a cloth or a mop. She didn't know what to do. Then her dog licked up the water for her!

2. Fran Miller doesn't want us to spill water.

Fran Miller wants us to have fun reading this story.

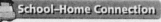

School-Home Connection

Talk about a story that you and your child know. Ask your child, "Why do you think the author wrote the story?"

Name ____________________

Phonics: Phonograms *-own, -oast*

Lesson 18

Write a word from the box to complete each sentence.

flown	roast	own
toast	grown	coast

1. Dad made ______________ and jam.

2. Then we went to the ______________.

3. We like to ______________ hot dogs.

4. I can help make my ______________ lunch.

5. I have ______________ up a lot.

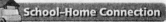

School-Home Connection

Have your child read each completed sentence aloud. Point to the word *flown* and ask your child to use it in a sentence.

Name ______________________________

▶ **Choose a pair of homophones from the chart. Write sentences using the words correctly.**

buy	by
to	two
wax	whacks

1. ______________________________

2. ______________________________

School-Home Connection
With your child, make flash cards of the words *by, buy, to, two, too, there, their,* and *they're.* Show each card, and have your child use the word correctly in a sentence.

Cut-Out/ Fold-Up Books

The chicks lived with Mom.
Soon they grew to be hens.

8

Chip, chip! A chick is out. It
hops a little and smells the air.

6

Fold

Fold

A Hen and Her Chicks

1

The hen needs some food.
She will not fly off and play.

3

"Cluck! Cluck!" says the hen.
Soon her eggs will hatch.

2

The hen calls to her friends.
"Come and see my little chicks!"

7

Fold

She checks the eggs and sits on
them. When will the eggs hatch?

4

She watches the eggs. Chip, chip!
An egg cracks!

5

Fold

Carla sells her stars.

8 That makes her feel happy.

Stars by Carla

1

Fold

"I make them," says Carla.

6 "You can hang them in your house."

Fold

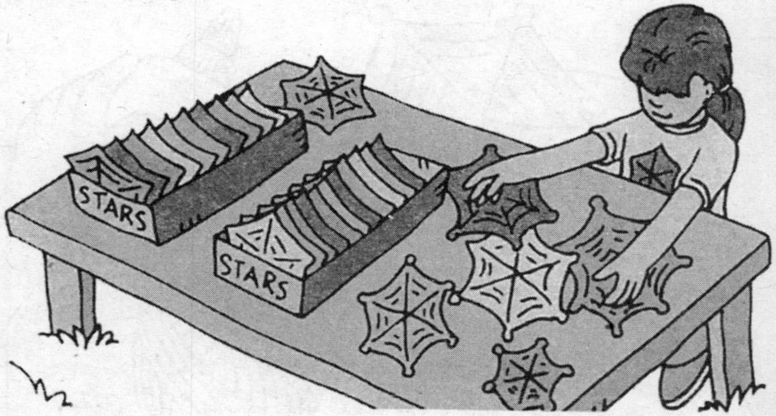

Carla makes stars at her house.

Then she puts them out to sell them. 3

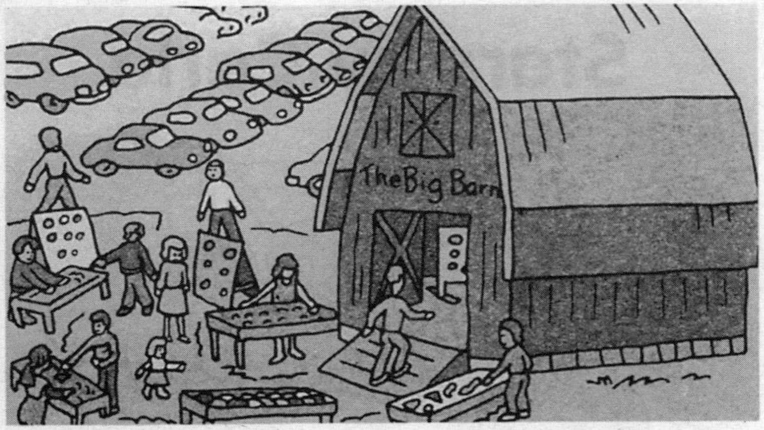

It's time for Craft Day again.
The cars park at the big barn.

2

"Can I get two? I know my
friend Bart will like one, too."

7

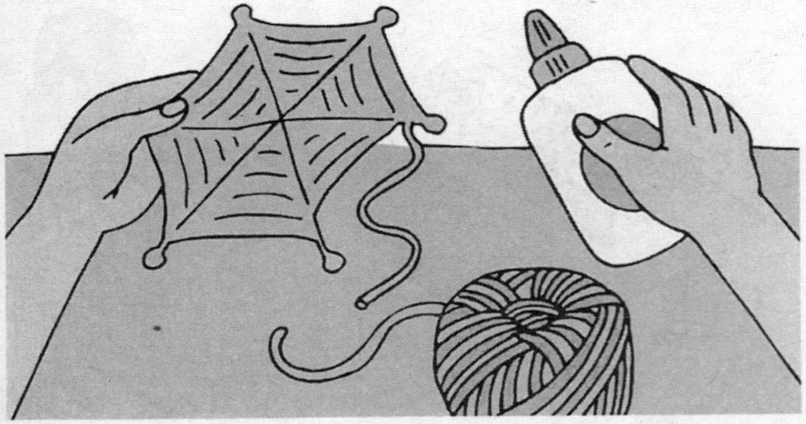

Sometimes the yarn slips
off a star. Carla fixes it.

4

"Who makes the stars?
What are they for?"

5

Fold

Fold

Ducks in the Night

1

"Look, Dad! What's that?
It must want to come in."

3

The ducks have finished their
bath. Quick! Let's get them out!

6

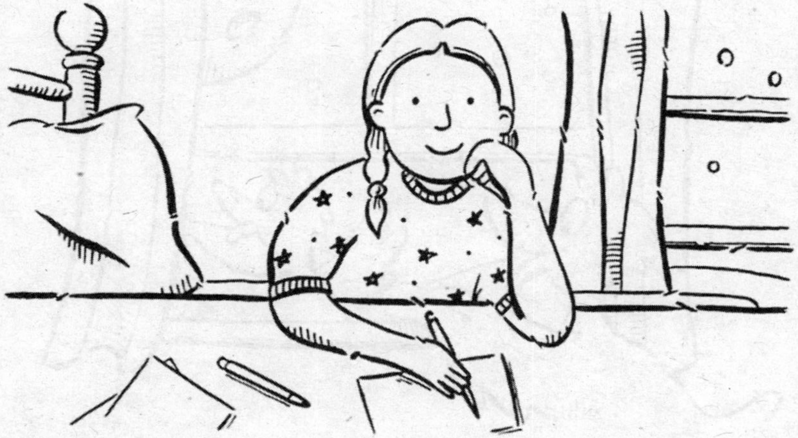

We had ducks in the house!
I am writing about that night.

8

Fold

Fold

My family is at home tonight. Mom makes a quilt. Dad and I read books.

2

Quack! Quack! Soon they are all out.

7

It's a bunch of ducks! What's this all about? Mom drops her quilt.

4

They are quacking in the bathtub! I think they grew up in a house.

5

Fold

Jump, Twirl, and Play

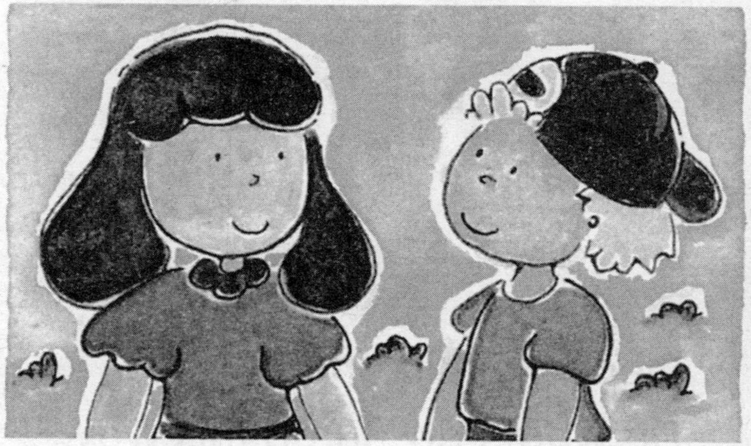

1

I always like to jump.
Can you jump like this?

3

Oh, no! We were twirling in the dirt. Now the dirt is on us.

6

Can you play the way we do?
Just don't twirl in the dirt!

8

Fold

Fold

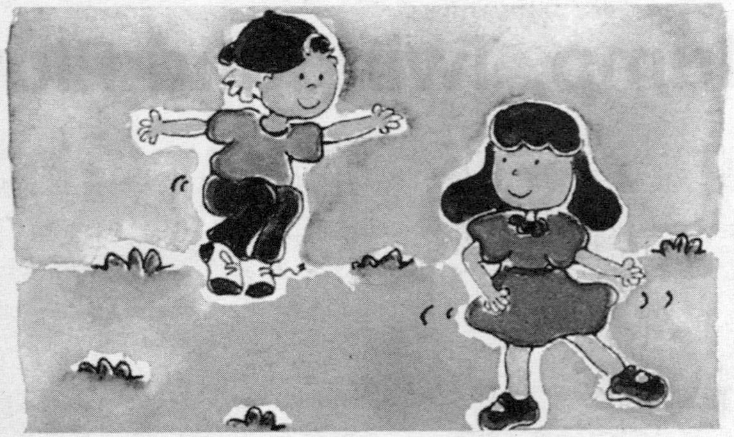

Please join in and play.
Do what I do. Jump this way.

2

The dirt is on my skirt.
The dirt is on my shirt.

7

Fold

Stand by me and take three jumps. Then turn and twirl.

4

There's lots of room to twirl and swirl. Jump this way and that.

5

Fold

Yes! I can play with a frog. It can
8 jump in puddles. Hi, little pet!

A turtle is nice. It could play
6 with me, but it can't jump.

Fold

A Pet for Me

1

I can carry my little bug,
and it can jump far. 3

Fold

2 I would like a pet that can jump.

Here is a pet you'll like.
It's home is very wet! 7

It's nice, but I am looking for some other pet. I would like one that can
4 play with me.

What about a turtle?
You can carry it to school. 5

Fold

Fold

Goat and Toad's Lunch

1

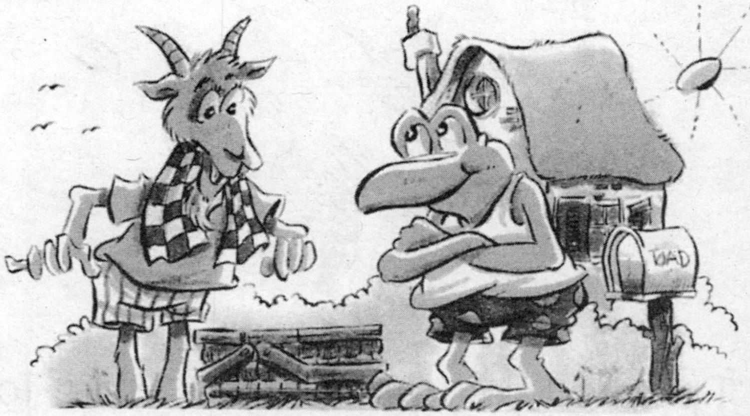

"What a load!" groaned Goat. "What did you pack for our lunch?"

3

The basket was harder and harder to lift. "Come on," said Toad. "Carry it over the hill."

6

Show the three surprises that you think were in the basket.

8

Fold

Fold

Goat met Toad for a picnic. "Let's go!"
said Toad. "I've packed lunch."

"I can't go any farther," said Goat.
"This is the best spot. Let's eat,"
said Toad.

Fold

"I packed a surprise lunch," said Toad.
Goat and Toad went down the road.
The sun glowed.

"What did you load into the
basket?" moaned Goat. "I put in
three nice things," croaked Toad.

Fold

Help Yourself

Characters

Horse 1 Horse 2 Man Bert Girl Brothers

It's raining! I just felt a drop on my head.

We are not far from an inn.

We need to stop there. I feel hungry for some good oats.

You're always hungry!

Why are the animals tossing their heads like that?

I think they felt the rain. Let's go! We are not far from a nice inn!

Watch out for that mud!

What mud?

Oh, no! That mud!

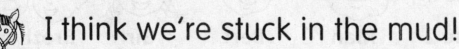

Let's go! We can't stop here.

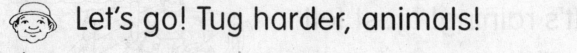

I think we're stuck in the mud!

Let's go! Tug harder, animals!

We're tugging! We're tugging!

I don't think he knows what you're saying.

Bert, get out and tug on the animals to get them going.

Don't tug on us. We are not stuck. The wagon is stuck!

Come along, animals. I'll tug on you, and you'll tug on the wagon.

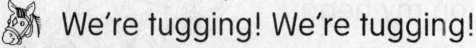

Tug, tug, tug, tug!

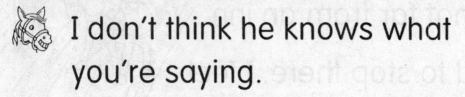

Let's go! Let's go!

No good. No good.

You look stuck!

Where did you come from?

Where did they come from?

That is our family's farm over there. Here are my brothers.

Hi!

How lucky that you showed up! Would you help us, please?

We could use some new people to help.

Yes, we can all help.

You go to the back. I will tug on the animals. They will tug on the wagon.

Let's go! Let's go!

Tug, Tug, Tug, Tug!

Work, work, work, work!

No good. No good.

Are there more people
in your family
who could help?

Please don't go back to your farm yet.
There is one other thing we did not
do yet.

What?

I could get down and help, too.

That could work.

Let's do it! I will help in the back.

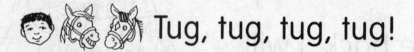

Tug, tug, tug, tug!

Work, work, work, work!

It's going!

Sometimes the
person missing
from the job is you.

Let's get to the inn!

Good luck!

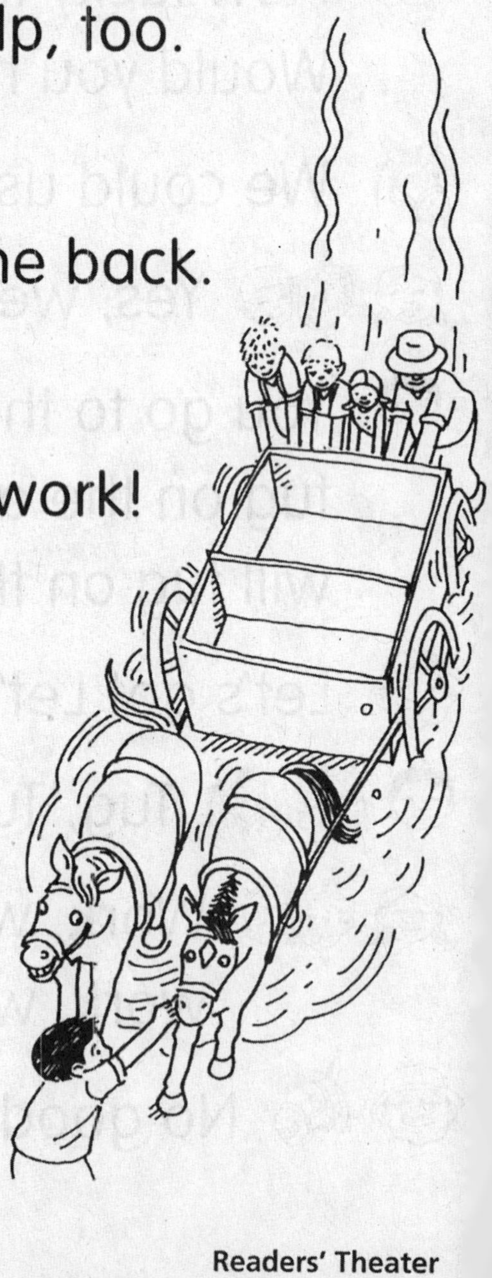

Make Your Mark

Book 1-4

Name ____________________

Circle the word that has the long e sound, as in wheel. Write the word to complete the sentence.

We They

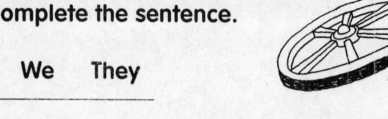

1. ____________ are digging in the garden.

like eat

2. Kim will ____________ all her lunch.

sleep rest

3. I ____________ in my bed.

peach food

4. This is a ____________.

good green

5. Kathleen sees a ____________ frog.

School-Home Connection

Have your child read each sentence aloud to you. Ask your child to think of other words with the long *e* sound, as in *we*.

Name ______________________________

▶ **Read the Spelling Words. Then write each word in the group where it belongs.**

Words with Long e

Words without Long e

Spelling Words

- me
- see
- feet
- seat
- mean
- team
- slow
- road
- our
- over

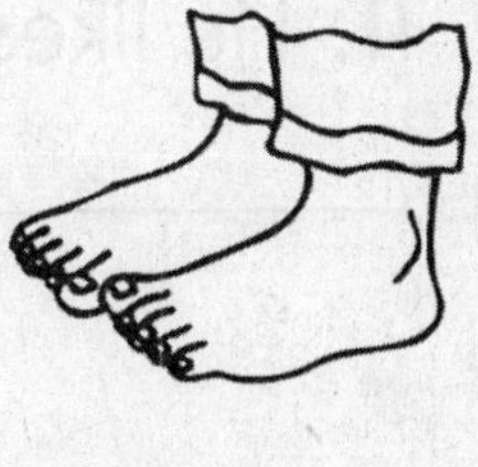

School-Home Connection

Have your child read each Spelling Word aloud. Ask your child to point to the words that have the long *e* sound, as in *we*.

Name ______________________

Write a word from the box to complete each sentence.

sweep	dream	reach	beach	sheep

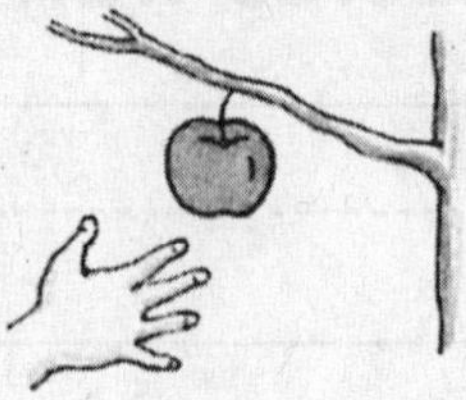

1. I ______________ for an apple.

2. Robert has a ______________.

3. Russ has a pet ______________.

4. He likes to ______________.

5. She is playing on the ______________.

School-Home Connection

Write the sentence, *"We need peas."* Ask your child to read the sentence and tell how the words are alike and different.

Name ______________________

▶ **Write a word from the box to complete each sentence.**

door	hurry	mother	dear
should	sky	told	

1. My ____________ and I are going to the park.

2. Mom locks the ____________ before we go.

3. I ____________ my friends we'd be there soon.

4. We ____________ ____________ to get there.

5. The ____________ is getting dark.

School-Home Connection

Have your child read the sentences aloud. Then ask your child to think of a sentence that uses more than one word from the box.

Look at the picture that shows what happened. Then circle the sentence that tells why it happened.

What Happened?	Why Did It Happen?
1. 	She likes to drink milk. She dropped the cup. Milk was in the cup.
2. 	His pillow was soft. He wanted to play. He was sick.
3. 	The snow is cold. It's fun to play outside. The snow melted in the sun.
4. 	They are sitting down. They liked the play. They will go home.

School-Home Connection

Talk about a story that you and your child have read. Have your child tell something that happened in the story and explain why it happened.

Name ______________________________

Read the chart. Then write the contraction that completes each sentence.

We	have	We've
You	are	You're
I	have	I've
We	are	We're
They	are	They're

1. Do you see them? ______________ fishing.

2. I am big. ______________ grown.

3. Please slow down. ______________ going too fast.

4. I like Jeff. ______________ good friends.

School-Home Connection
Cover the second column of the chart, and have your child tell you the contraction for each pair of words.

Name ____________________

▶ **Write two sentences that tell about things in the picture. Use describing words in each sentence.**

1. ____________________

2. ____________________

School-Home Connection

Play *I Spy* with your child using words that tell about color, size, and shape. For example, *I spy something small, round, and yellow.* (a lemon)

Name ______________________________

Write the word from the box that completes the sentence.

way	sway	birthday	paint	rainbow	chain

1. Today is Peg's ________________.

2. Look at the pretty ________________.

3. The trees ________________ in the wind.

4. This is the shortest ________________.

5. Doris needs yellow ________________.

School–Home Connection

Have your child read each completed sentence aloud. Point to the word *chain* in the box, and ask him or her to use the word in a sentence.

Name ______________________________

▶ Write a word from the box to complete the sentence.

cool	dry	four	holes	move	place	warm

1. I stay ____________ in my winter jacket.

2. My raincoat keeps me ____________ when it rains.

3. My shorts keep my legs ____________ in summer.

4. I dig ____________ in the sand.

5. I like the ____________ where I live.

Try This

Write a sentence that uses the word four.

School-Home Connection

Have your child read the sentences aloud. Encourage him or her to write a new sentence that includes two words from the box.

Name ______________________________

The picture shows what happened.

Write a sentence that tells why it happened.

He ran inside.

She fed the rabbit.

The paint spilled.

School-Home Connection

Talk about a story that your child enjoys. Have your child tell you something that happened in the story and explain why it happened.

Name ______________________

Cross out the word that is wrong. Write the correct word that ends with <u>ail</u> or <u>aid</u>.

1. Fay reads her mall.

2. Lee brings the pal to the barn.

3. I see a snake.

4. The man got pod.

5. The dog wants to catch his tall.

6. I have a brad.

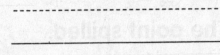

School-Home Connection
Say a sentence with one incorrect word. Have your child say the sentence correctly.

Name ______________________

Use describing words to write a sentence about each picture. Write the sentences correctly.

1.

2.

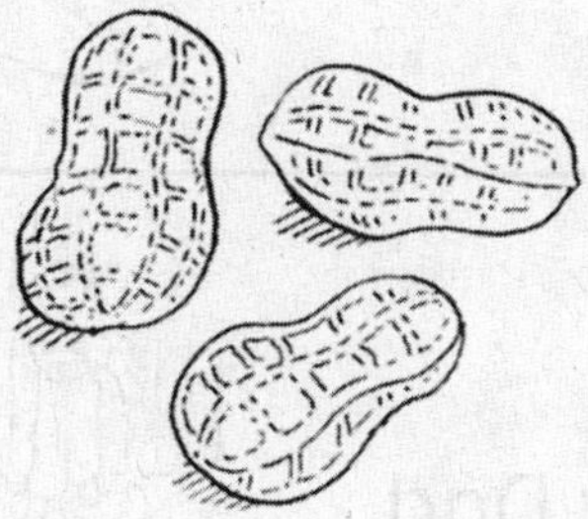

3.

School–Home Connection

Talk to your child, using words that describe what things taste, smell, sound, and feel like (*salty, fresh, squeaky, sharp*). Have your child identify each describing word you use.

Name ______________________________

▶ Write the word from the box that completes the sentence.

came	gate	gave	lake
paste	scale	shade	take

1. I helped Dad paint the ____________.

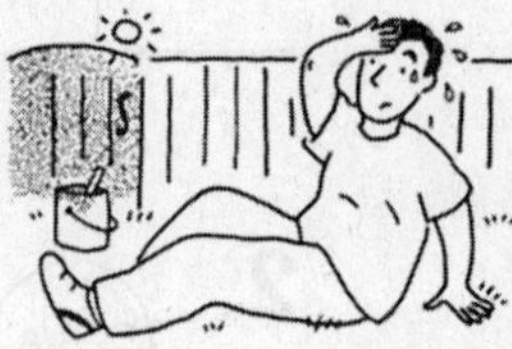

2. Dad had to ____________ a rest.

3. I ____________ over to sit near Dad.

4. We sat in the ____________.

5. Dad ____________ me a cold drink.

School-Home Connection

Point to the words *lake*, *scale*, and *paste*. Have your child write each word in a sentence.

Name ______________________________

► **Read the Spelling Words. Then write each word in the group where it belongs.**

Spelling Words

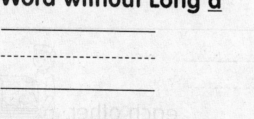

- came
- game
- gate
- late
- lake
- take
- day
- play
- four
- place

Words with Long a

______________ ______________

______________ ______________

______________ ______________

______________ ______________

______________ ______________

____

Word without Long a

____

School-Home Connection

Write the Spelling Word *came*, and ask your child to change one letter to make the Spelling Word *game*. Repeat with *gate* (*late*) and *lake* (*take*).

Name ______________________

Write the word from the box that completes the sentence.

chase	gave	late
name	paste	wake

1. It's time for my brother to ____________ up.

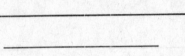

2. This is not a day to sleep ____________.

3. Last night, our uncle ____________ us two hamsters.

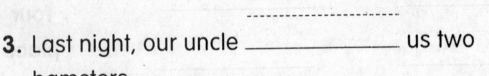

4. I want to ____________ my hamster Jake.

5. We watch them ____________ each other.

School-Home Connection
Have your child read each completed sentence aloud. Then write the words *cap* and *cape*. Have your child read each word and draw a picture for it.

Name ____________________

▶ Write a word from the box to complete the sentence.

around	found	near	tired
might	open	gone	hears

1. Snake ____________ a loud crash.

2. He looks ____________ the classroom.

3. Snake has ____________ spilled paint.

4. It ____________ take all night to clean up.

5. Snake cleans up. Now he is ____________!

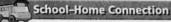

School-Home Connection

Have your child read each completed sentence aloud. Then ask him or her to write these words in other sentences.

Name ____________________

Read about each problem. Then circle the better solution.

1. Kate's doll always gets lost. On some days, she finds it under the bed. On other days, she can't find it at all.

Kate could put the doll on a shelf.

Kate could give the doll to her sister.

2. Dave eats popcorn. He drops it all over the place. Popcorn is on the rug.

Dave should eat crackers, too.

Dave should clean up the popcorn.

3. Edmund's dog jumps up on people. It will not sit when Edmund tells it to sit. It barks all the time, too.

Edmund needs to get a bigger dog.

Edmund needs to train his dog.

School-Home Connection

Talk about a problem in a story you and your child have read. Talk about how the problem was solved.

Name ______________________

Write the word from the box that completes the sentence.

plane	shade	Shane
made	cane	lane

1. A hat and a ____________ are by the door.

2. Blake ____________ a sandwich for lunch.

3. Blake will eat his sandwich on the ____________.

4. They sit in the ____________.

5. Uncle ____________ waves at them.

School-Home Connection

Have your child read each completed sentence aloud. Together, think of other words that end in *-ane* and *-ade*.

Name ______________________________

▶ **Look at the picture. Write sentences that tell what you see. Use words that tell how many.**

____

1. ______________________________

____

2. ______________________________

____

3. ______________________________

____

4. ______________________________

____

5. ______________________________

School-Home Connection

Play a game with your child describing things you see nearby. Use words that tell how many. Have your child guess what you are describing.

Name ____________________

▶ **Read about each problem. Then circle the better solution.**

1. Kim is cleaning her room. She put all her things in the box. Now she can't shut the lid.

Kim could take some things out.
Kim could stop cleaning her room.

---

2. Mike likes to read in school. He likes to read at home, too. Mike has too many books to carry. He keeps dropping the books.

Mike could read the books.
Mike could get a backpack.

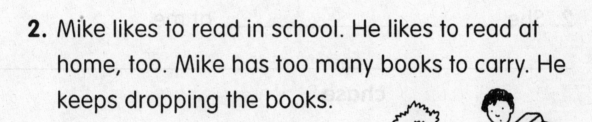

3. Jill has on a new dress. It is raining. Jill wants to keep her dress dry.

Jill could put on her raincoat.
Jill could sing about rain.

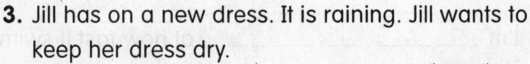

School–Home Connection
Talk about a story you and your child have read in which there was a problem. Help your child recall how the problem was solved.

Name ______________________________

Add -ed or -ing to make a new word.
Write the word to complete the sentence.

wave

____

1. My friend ______________________ to me.

smile

____

2. She ______________________ at me.

chase

____

3. I am ______________________ a little fish.

surprise

____

4. I'm ______________________ at how fast it swims.

nibble

____

5. The fish are ______________________ my feet!

School-Home Connection

Have your child read each completed sentence aloud. Ask him or her which letter in each word was dropped when *–ed* and *–ing* were added.

Name ______________________

▶ Complete the sentences with feeling words.

1. When I play, I feel ____________.

2. When I get a gift, I am ____________.

3. When I sing a song, I feel ____________.

▶ Write sentences to describe each picture. Use feeling words.

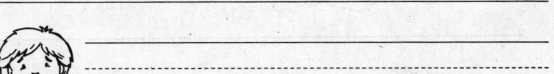

4. 

____

____

5. 

____

____

School-Home Connection

Ask your child to draw simple faces that show feelings. Then create sentences that describe those feelings.

Name ____________________

Circle the sentence that tells about each picture.

1. 

Kathleen hops in a game.

Kathleen hopes to play well.

2. 

Mom has a soft brown robe.

Mom has a brown stone.

3. 

This note is for you.

This net is for you.

4. 

There are holes here.

There are halls in here.

5. 

She woke up at ten.

She walked at ten.

School-Home Connection

Have your child read each sentence aloud. Ask which words have the long *o* sound as in *hope*.

Name ____________________

▶ Read the Spelling Words. Then write each word in the group where it belongs.

Spelling Words
- home
- hope
- rope
- rode
- rose
- those
- like
- nine
- right
- walk

Words with Long o

____________________ ____________________

____________________ ____________________

____________________ ____________________

____________________ ____________________

____________________ ____________________

____________________ ____________________

Words without Long o

____________________ ____________________

____________________ ____________________

____________________ ____________________

____________________ ____________________

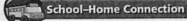

School-Home Connection

Have your child read each Spelling Word aloud. Talk about how the words are alike and how they are different. Start by comparing *home* and *hope*.

Name ______________________

Complete each sentence with a word that has the long o sound, as in rope.

froze	broke	rose	globe	spoke	hole

1. 

Ann ______________ the vase.

2. 

Do you see land on the ______________?

3. 

The water in the pond ______________.

4. 

He found a ______________ in his sock.

5. 

Kay smells the ______________.

School–Home Connection

Ask your child to read one of the sentences he or she completed. Talk about how the words in the box are alike and how they are different.

Name ____________________

Write a word from the box to complete each sentence.

brown	hello	loudly
love	pulled	city

1. My family rode the bus to the ____________.

2. The bus driver said ____________ to us.

3. The bus ____________ into the bus stop.

4. I ____________ to look in all the store windows.

5. Cars honked their horns ____________.

School-Home Connection

Have your child read each completed sentence aloud. Ask him or her to write another sentence for this story, using the word *brown*.

Name ______________________________________

Read the story. Look at the picture. Circle the sentence that draws a conclusion about the story.

1. Rose is very happy. She is thinking of the big cake she will have. Rose giggles when she thinks about the gifts she will open.

Rose must feed her cat.

It is Rose's birthday.

2. Kevin wore his green shirt to school. He put on green socks, too. Kevin wants a green rug for his room.

Kevin likes green.

Kevin likes frogs.

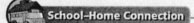

School-Home Connection

Give your child some clues about someone or something in the house. Ask your child to name the person or thing. Then have your child give you clues.

Name ____________________

▶ **Circle the word that completes the sentence. Then write the word.**

bone **bean**

1. The dog has a ____________________.

throne **mole**

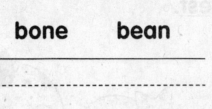

2. The king sits on his ____________________.

tone **tadpole**

3. I see a little ____________________.

heal **hole**

4. Ben is digging a ____________________ for his plant.

stone **stain**

5. She is painting on the ____________________.

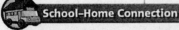

School-Home Connection

Together, think of other words that end in *one* and *ole*.

Name ______________________________

Look at the picture. Write sentences that compare the animals. Use words that end in er and est.

1. ______________________________

2. ______________________________

3. ______________________________

School-Home Connection

Write the words *tall, taller,* and *tallest*. Have your child read each word and then draw a picture that illustrates it.

Name ____________________

▶ **Write the words where they belong in the puzzle.**

cage	bridge	mice
pages	prince	space

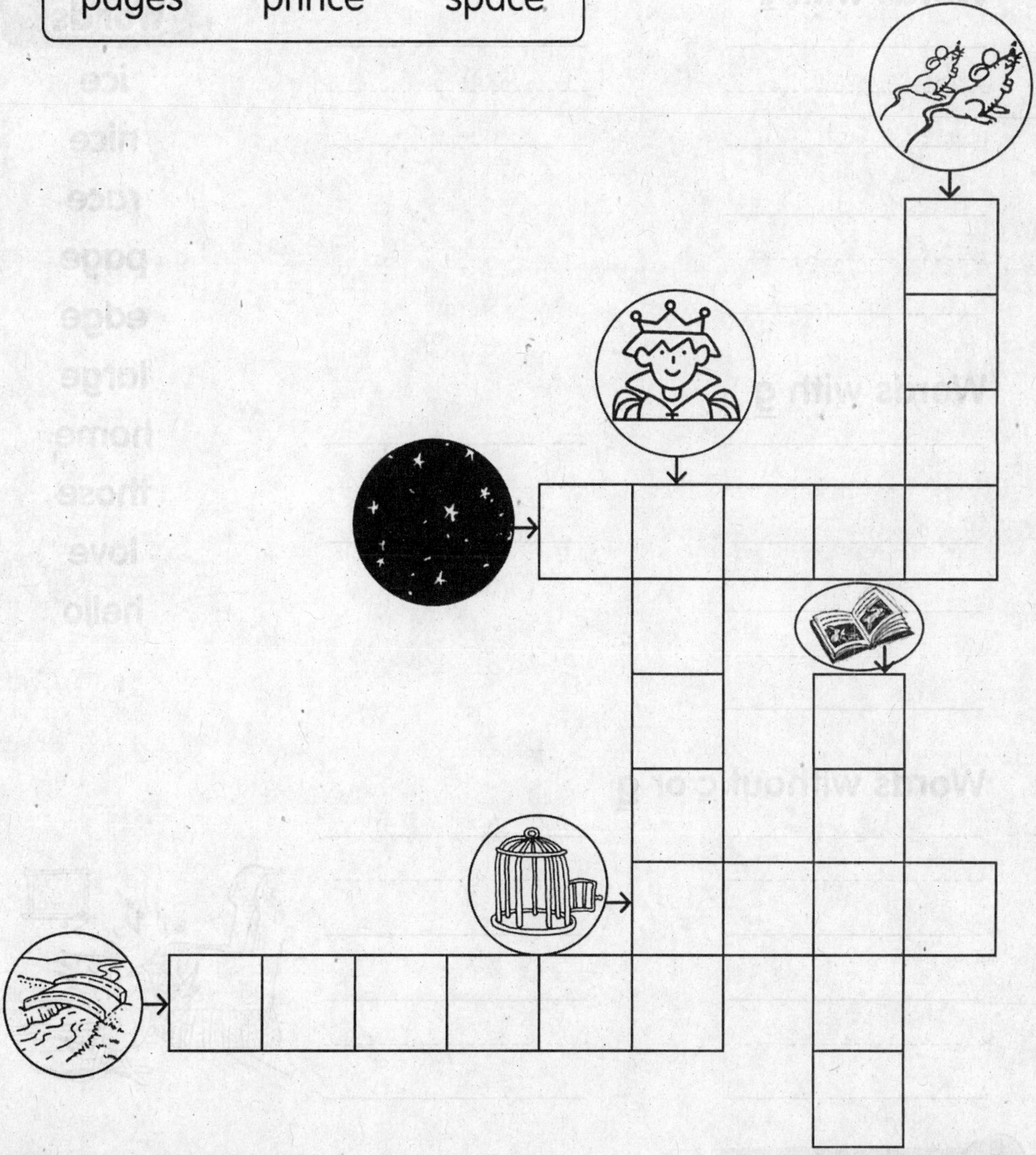

School–Home Connection

Write the words *circus*, *fudge*, and *germ*. Give a clue for each word, and have your child point to the correct word.

Name ______________________________

Read the Spelling Words. Then write each word in the group where it belongs.

Spelling Words

- ice
- nice
- race
- page
- edge
- large
- home
- those
- love
- hello

Words with c

________________ ________________

____

____

Words with g

________________ ________________

____

____

Words without c or g

________________ ________________

________________ ________________

________________ ________________

School-Home Connection

Have your child circle the *d* in the word spelled with *dge*. (*edge*) Then ask him or her to put a checkmark by all the words that end in silent *e*. (all words except *hello*)

Name ______________________

Write the word from the box that completes the sentence.

stage	danced	fudge
center	gentle	circus

1. Ginger went to a __________ with her dad.

2. They ate __________ at the show.

3. The show was in the __________.

4. The people were on the __________.

5. People __________ on a wire.

School-Home Connection

Have your child read each completed sentence aloud. Then ask him or her to write a sentence using the word *gentle*.

Name ______________________________

Write a word from the box to complete the sentence.

eyes	listen	visitor	remembered
become	talk	busy	high

1. Mom was ______________ baking a cake.

2. She put the cake up ______________ to cool off.

3. Spot had ______________ excited about the cake.

4. Just then, a ______________ rang the doorbell.

5. Mom ______________ Spot. It was too late!

School-Home Connection

Have your child read each completed sentence aloud. Together, make up sentences for the unused words in the box.

Name ______________________________

▶ **Read the story. Look at the picture. Circle the sentence that draws a conclusion about the story.**

1. Jade feeds Hank, her hamster, and gives him fresh water. When Hank is asleep, she reads about cats and dogs.

Hank reads many books.

Jade likes animals very much.

---

2. Tim and Neal jump into the water. It is cold! Dennis goes down the slide. "Neal, I like to play in your pool!" Dennis says.

The boys are swimming at Neal's house.

Neal and his friends can't swim well.

---

3. Nick and Dad hang a note at the store. The note says Lost cat, black with white feet. Nick says to Dad, "I hope he will be found. I miss him so much."

Nick does not like cats.

Nick feels sad.

School-Home Connection

Talk with your child about the answer that he or she chose for each story. Ask your child to explain some of the clues that helped him or her choose the answer.

Name ______________________________

▶ **Write the contraction that completes the sentence.**

can't	didn't	We'll
Mom's	Dad's	He'll

1. ______________ go to the lake to camp.

2. My friend ______________ come with us.

3. ______________ come with us next time.

4. ______________ packing the bags.

5. ______________ taking the bags to the car.

School-Home Connection
Ask your child to point out the contraction that was not used. (*didn't*) Then have him or her tell you the two words that make up the contraction.

Name ______________________________

▶ **Draw pictures to show two meanings of each word. Choose one meaning, and write a sentence that shows it.**

1. bump

2. wave

School–Home Connection
With your child, think of sentences for two meanings of the word *watch*. Have your child draw a picture for each meaning of the word.

Cut-Out/ Fold-Up Books

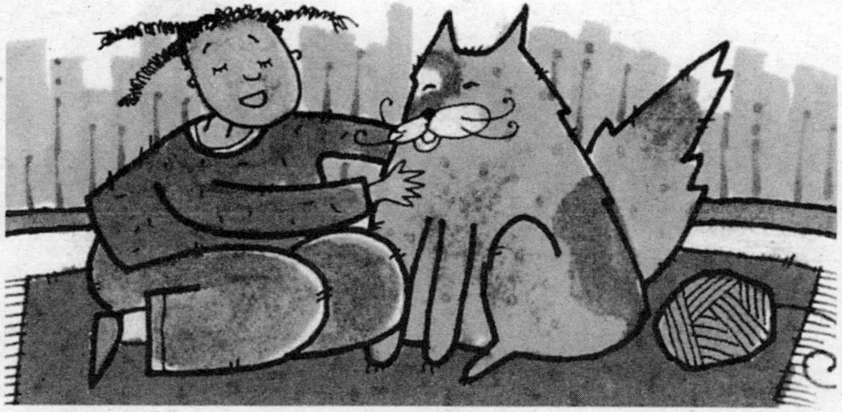

"Hurry Patch," said Doreen, "let's go home. I'll feed you a treat."

8

Can I Keep Him?

1

"Dad, may I keep him?" asked Doreen. "Yes," said Dad. "You need a pet."

6

"Mother told me I could keep one. I will keep this one," said Jean.

3

Fold

Fold

Jean saw two cats by her house.
They did not have a home.

2

"He needs a name," said Dad.
"Let's call him Patch."

7

Fold

"This is a nice cat, too. I should
ask Doreen if she wants a cat."

4

Doreen wants the cat. "Oh, dear!"
Doreen said. "I hope my dad will
let me keep him."

5

Then the two friends played
8 all day.

Work, Then Play

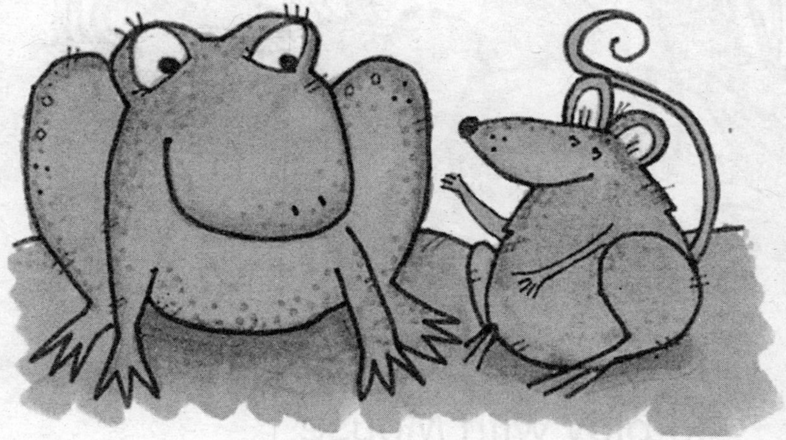

1

"Make a warm, dry home.
6 Then you may play."

Mouse said she could not play.
She had to make a place to live. 3

One warm day, Frog wanted to play with Mouse.

2

There were just four more days until winter. Soon it would be very cool outside.

4

Fold

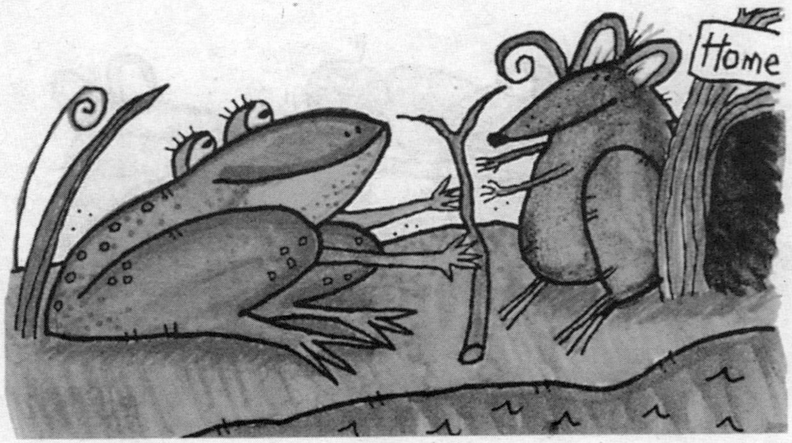

Frog helped Mouse make her home. At last, her home was finished.

7

Her Dad said, "Mouse, you must make a winter home."

5

Fold

People like to watch the players
step up to the plate and hit the ball.
8 CRACK!

People in many lands play the
game. They play in the same way—
6 with a ball, a bat, and a mitt.

1

3

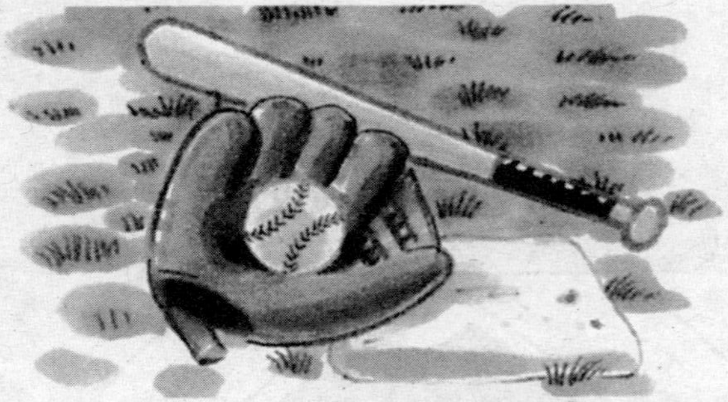

People play baseball in many places. To play the game, you need only a ball, a bat, a mitt, and a big place to play.

2

People might get tired when they play baseball. You have to run around a lot.

7

Fold

The game began in the U.S.A. First, it was called town ball. Then it became baseball.

4

5

Fold

Bird Tales

1

One bird finds worms. Those worms are good for dinner.

3

He wants to fly away again. Where will he go?

6

Four white birds think about the new tales they will hear.

8

Fold

Fold

Five white birds live in the same nest. They get along because they're friends.

2

One bird tells tales about the places he has seen.

4

He doesn't know. He will come right back to tell more tales.

7

The others like to hear his tales. They smile because his tales are good.

5

Fold

Fold

Bones ate up the toast and jam. All I got was a mess to clean up!

8

Bad Dog!

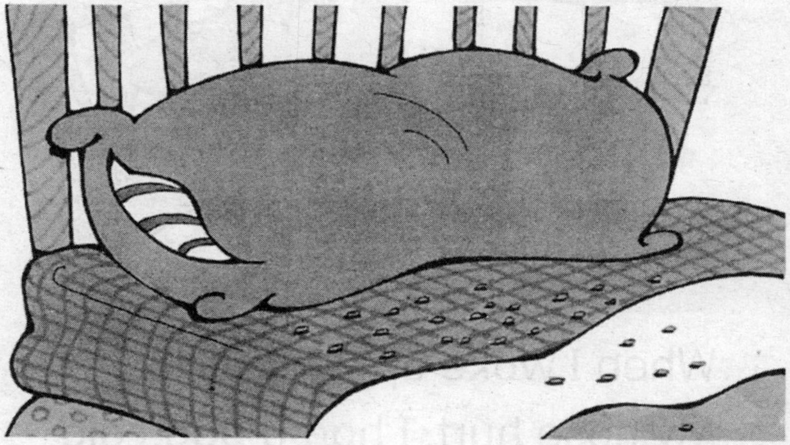

1

"I hope you will get down now, Bones!" said Jake.

6

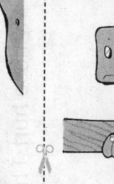

"Hello," said Jake. "Do you want toast with jam?"

3

Fold

Fold

When I woke up, I felt sick.
My nose hurt. I had a bad cold.

2

Bones jumped and poked around.
Then he barked loudly.

7

Fold

"Yes, I'd love toast with jam,"
I said.

4

My dog, Bones, jumped up and pulled the blanket. "No!" I said loudly.

5

Fold

The Old Bridge

1

"Let's try to cross the old bridge," said the little goat to the larger goats. "No!" they said. "Rage won't let us!" 3

6 "Just look at this rail," said the little goat. "It's not safe."

By now, the little goat had crossed the bridge. "Good-bye, Rage!" he called.
8 "Have fun fixing your bridge!"

Fold

Rage sat on his old bridge.
"Listen, everyone! This is my bridge.
2 I will let no one cross it!"

"Let's talk, Rage," said the little goat.
"You need to fix your bridge." "I do not!"
4 yelled Rage. "Go away!"

Fold

"Open your eyes, Rage! Look at this
large space in the center." 7

"This bridge has become old," said
the little goat. "Look at this edge.
It needs paint." 5

Fold

The Princess and the Peas

Narrator	**King Jack**	**Queen Jane**
Prince Ken	**King Dan**	**Princess Pam**

Narrator: In a land far away lived Queen Jane and King Jack. They were always looking for new friends for their son, Prince Ken.

Prince Ken: My friends must be smart and kind. They must also have good manners.

King Jack: We want you to have good manners, too.

Narrator: One day the doorbell rang. Prince Ken opened the door. The visitors were King Dan and Princess Pam.

King Jack: Hello! Please come in.

King Dan: What a lovely, warm place you have here.

Queen Jane: King Dan has very nice manners. Let's see if Princess Pam does, too.

Princess Pam: My mother asked me to bring you these flowers, Queen Jane.

Queen Jane: Thank you! They are so pretty!

Narrator: The king and queen invited King Dan and Princess Pam to stay for dinner.

Queen Jane: Does Princess Pam like peas, King Dan?

King Dan: No, but I love peas. Peas with dinner will be fine.

Narrator: At dinner, everything was going very well.

Queen Jane: Would you like some milk, Princess Pam?

Princess Pam: Yes, please.

King Jack: Would you like more hot dogs, Princess Pam?

Princess Pam: No, thank you. I'm full, but they were very good, sir.

Queen Jane: You have such nice manners!

Narrator: The queen was watching to see if Princess Pam would try the peas. A person with good manners tries a bite of everything.

Princess Pam: Prince Ken, do you play basketball?

Prince Ken: Yes, I do! Do you play, too?

Princess Pam: I'm on a team.

Prince Ken: We should play a game after dinner.

Princess Pam: I would love to!

Narrator: Just then Princess Pam ate some peas.

King Jack: She's eating some peas!

Queen Jane: You don't like peas, but you still ate some!

King Jack: At last we've found the right friend for our son!

Prince Ken: Yes! Princess Pam is smart, kind, and she has good manners.

Princess Pam: Thank you! Would you like to play basketball now, Prince Ken?

Prince Ken: Yes! Let's go.

Narrator: That's how the princess who ate peas became Prince Ken's best friend.

Watch This!

Book 1-5

Name ______________________________

Circle the sentence that tells about the picture.

1. 

She thinks the doll is cute.

She thinks the doll is cut.

2. 

We like to go swimming in the tub.

We like to go swimming in June.

3. 

The cold cup is melting in the heat.

The ice cube is melting in the heat.

4. 

She shows us a cobweb.

She shows off her costume.

5. 

The tube is not empty.

The tub is not empty.

School-Home Connection

Have your child read each sentence aloud. Ask which words have the long *u* sound as in *cute*.

Name ______________________________

Read the Spelling Words. Then write each word in the group where it belongs.

Spelling Words

use
cute
cube
tube
tune
rule
nice
large
hear
talk

Words with u

______________ ______________
______________ ______________
______________ ______________
______________ ______________

Words without u

______________ ______________
______________ ______________
______________ ______________

School-Home Connection

Have your child read each Spelling Word aloud. Ask him or her to point to the Spelling Words that end with a silent *e*.

Name ______________________

Look at each picture. Write the word from the box that completes the sentence.

use	rude	cute	flute	cube	mule

1. The block is the shape of a ____________.

2. Jake plays the ____________ well.

3. The ____________ will not get up.

4. She will ____________ the brush.

5. He holds the ____________ kitten.

School-Home Connection

Write the words *hug* and *huge*. Have your child read the words aloud. Talk about how the words are alike and different.

Name ______________________________

Write the word from the box to complete the sentence.

clear	color	good-bye	hair
kinds	toes	only	

1. We saw all ______________ of animals.

2. A cat was licking between her ______________.

3. I saw fish in a ______________ tank.

4. Dad liked the green ______________ of the little bird.

5. I saw ______________ one cat.

Try This

Write a sentence using a word from the box.

School-Home Connection

Have your child read the words and sentences aloud. Encourage your child to write other sentences using the words.

Name ______________________

Comprehension: Alphabetize

Lesson 25

▶ Put the words in ABC order.

pond	fish	swim	duck

1. ______________ 2. ______________

3. ______________ 4. swim

hide	bird	flip	spray

1. ______________ 2. flip

3. ______________ 4. ______________

School-Home Connection

Ask your child to read aloud the words in each box. Have your child explain how he or she put the words in order.

Name ______________________

▶ **Add ed or ing to the word. Write the new word in the sentence. Remember to drop the e or double the last letter.**

1. I ______________ my mom and dad good-bye.

hug

2. My big brother and I went ______________.

hike

3. We ______________ at the stars last night.

gaze

4. Today, we will be ______________ up rocks.

dig

5. We are ______________ lots of fun!

have

School-Home Connection

Point to the words *hug* and *hike*. Ask your child to explain how each word changes when *ing* or *ed* is added to it.

Name ______________________________

▶ Use verbs from the box. Write sentences that tell what animals do.

leap	jump	wiggle	lick
bite	paddle	swim	dive
slither	sleep	cuddle	gobble
flop			

1. ______________________________

2. ______________________________

3. ______________________________

School–Home Connection

Say sentences aloud using interesting verbs such as *wiggle, bump, stretch, crumple, freeze,* and *shuffle*. Have your child identify the verb in each sentence.

Name ________________________________

▶ **Circle the word that completes the sentence. Then write the word.**

pea pie pay

1. Beaver was eating some ____________.

try tray tie

2. "May I ____________ some of that?" asked Turtle.

mitt mate might

3. "You ____________ not like it," said Beaver.

Way Why We

4. "____________ not?" asked Turtle.

may me my

5. "I make ____________ pies with mud," Beaver said.

School-Home Connection

Have your child read each sentence aloud. Ask which words have the long *i* sound.

Name ______________________________

▶ **Read the Spelling Words. Then write each word in the group where it belongs.**

Spelling Words

- my
- try
- tried
- ties
- light
- might
- use
- rule
- hair
- color

Words with i

______________ ______________

______________ ______________

______________ ______________

____

Words with y

______________ ______________

Words without i or y

______________ ______________

______________ ______________

____

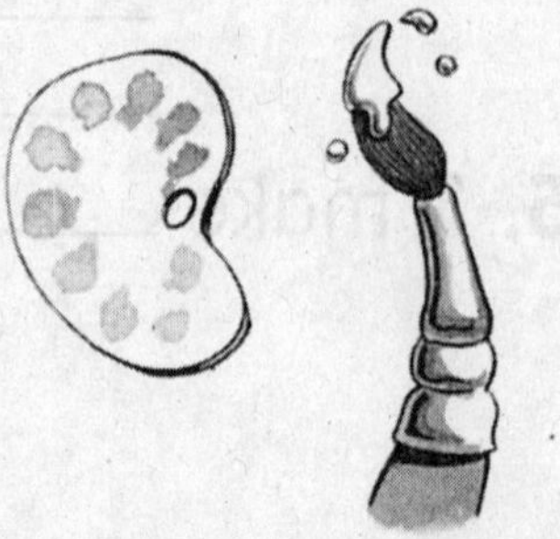

School-Home Connection

Have your child read each Spelling Word aloud. Talk about different ways to spell the sound /ī/.

Name ______________________________

Write the word from the box that completes the sentence.

cried	high	lights	night
sight	sky	tried	why

1. Last ______________, we looked at the stars.

2. It was fun to see their twinkling ______________.

3. "There's a falling star!" ______________ Mom.

4. "What a lovely ______________!"

5. She reached out and ______________ to catch it.

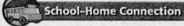

School-Home Connection

Have your child read the words and sentences aloud. Encourage him or her to write additional sentences using the words *high* and *why*.

Name ______________________

▶ **Write the word from the box that completes the sentence.**

climbed	earth	fooling	thought	table

1. We will read about the ______________.

2. Luke ______________ that he would like to read about that.

3. Mrs. Hill ______________ up to get the globe.

4. She set the large globe on the ______________.

5. Mrs. Hill was not ______________ us when she told us the earth is round!

School-Home Connection

Point to each word in the box, and have your child use it in a sentence.

Name ________________________________

Read the story. Then circle the answer to each question.

The sun is shining on the creek. Beaver is cutting down a small tree. He is making a nice home out of sticks and branches.

Beaver hears some children playing nearby. Splash! Beaver slaps his flat tail on the water. This tells all the beavers to hide until the children go away.

Chomp, chomp! Nibble, nibble! Beaver must hurry. At the end of the day, Beaver has a nice new home.

1. Who is this story about?
   some children Beaver a tree

2. Where does this story happen?
   at a creek in a house at a school

3. What is it about?
   - Children like to play by creeks and look at beavers.
   - Beavers can slap their tails on the water.
   - Beaver works hard and makes a nice home.

School-Home Connection

Have your child read the story aloud. Talk about what happens in the beginning, in the middle, and at the end of the story.

Name ______________________________

Look at the picture. Write the word from the box that completes the sentence.

She'd	They're	He'd	You'd	We've	I've

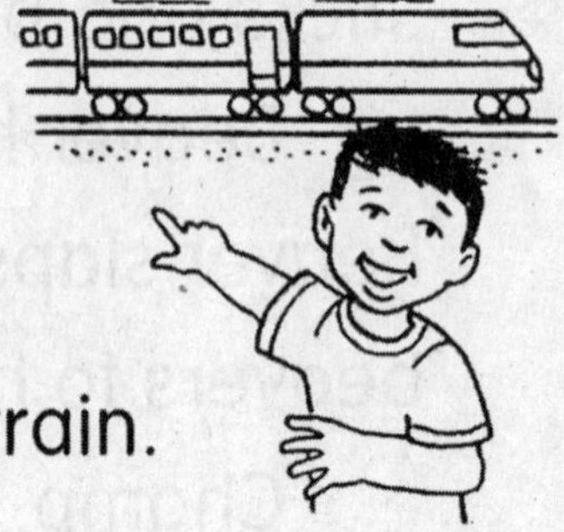

1. ______________ like to ride on the train.

2. ______________ having fun sailing on the lake.

3. ______________ lost my hamster. Will you help me find it?

4. ______________ like to swim with the other children.

School-Home Connection

Ask your child to read one of the sentences he or she completed. Then ask your child what two words make up each contraction.

Name ______________________________

▶ **Use verbs from the chart to write sentences that tell about now.**

plant	grow	fall	dig	pick
plants	grows	falls	digs	picks

1. ______________________________

____

2. ______________________________

____

3. ______________________________

____

School-Home Connection

With your child, make up sentences using the verbs *stamp*, *shake*, and *sweep*. Then ask your child to add *s* to each verb and use it in a new sentence.

Name ________________________

Write the word from the box that completes each sentence.

tower	proud	crown
flowers	found	out

1. The queen put her ____________ on.

2. She went ____________ to find the king.

3. The king could not be ____________.

4. She went up in the ____________.

5. She saw the king picking ____________.

School–Home Connection

Have your child read each completed sentence aloud. Point to the word *proud*, and ask your child to use the word in a sentence.

Name ____________________

▶ **Read the Spelling Words. Then write each word in the group where it belongs.**

Words with ow

____________________ ____________________

____

____

Words with ou

____________________ ____________________

____________________ ____________________

____

Words without ow or ou

____________________ ____________________

____________________ ____________________

____________________ ____________________

Spelling Words

how
cow
down
out
found
round
try
light
earth
table

School-Home Connection

Ask your child to read aloud two pairs of Spelling Words that rhyme. (*how, cow; found, round*) Have your child think of words to rhyme with the other Spelling Words.

Name ________________________________

Write the words where they belong in the puzzle.

couch	cow	house	flower
mouth	owl	tower	

1. 
2. 
3. 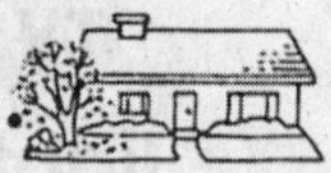
4. 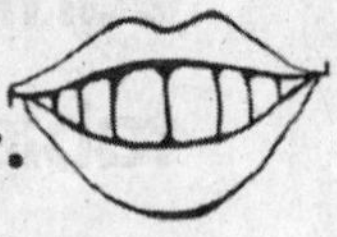
5. 
6. 
7. 

School–Home Connection

Write the words *blouse*, *growl*, *cloud*, and *round*. Say a clue for each word, and have your child point to the correct word.

Name ______________________

▶ Write a word from the box to complete each sentence.

answered	baby	heard	pools
done	pushed	together	

1. Mrs. Brown ______________ the door.

2. We went to the park ______________.

3. Mrs. Brown's ______________ went too.

4. I ______________ Brad on the swing.

5. We ______________ Brad giggle.

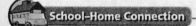

School-Home Connection

Ask your child to find the word *pools* in the box. Ask him or her to use it in a sentence.

Read the story. Then circle the best answer for each question.

Butterfly woke up and said, "I am going on a trip to see my friends!" He packed a snack.

Up, up, up he flew. "Oh no!" Butterfly cried. "I forgot my map! How will I find my friends?"

Butterfly tried to think of what to do. He said, "I will look for the bright red flowers in their yard!" He saw the flowers. He flew down.

"Hi, Robin! I'm so glad to be here!" Butterfly called.

1. Who is this story about?

   Robin and Finch **Butterfly** **birds**

2. When does the story happen?

   at lunchtime **in the night** **in the morning**

3. What is the story about?

   Butterfly eats a snack.

   Butterfly wants to find his friends.

   Butterfly sets things up for a game.

School-Home Connection

Ask your child to read the story to you. Talk about what happens in the beginning, middle, and ending of the story.

Name ________________________

Write the word from the box that completes each sentence.

ground	town	round
sound	down	clown

1. Ed dressed up like a ________________ for my birthday.

2. He jumped up and ________________.

3. He fell on the ________________ and giggled.

4. His dog played with a ________________ ball.

5. Ed is the best clown in ________________!

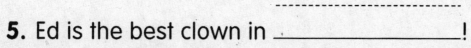

School–Home Connection

Have your child read each completed sentence aloud. Point to the word *sound*, and ask him or her to say it in a sentence.

Name ______________________________

Write am, is, or are to complete each sentence.

1. I ________ riding my bike.

2. Mom ________ riding her bike.

3. We ________ riding to the pond.

4. You ________ going too fast!

5. She ________ waiting for me.

School-Home Connection

Help your child use *am, is,* and *are* correctly. Say what you are doing—for example, *I am cutting carrots. This carrot is long.* Have your child create similar sentences.

Name ______________________________

▶ Circle the sentence that tells about each picture.

1. The pets hurry to a field.
   We're having a funny pet party.

2. Annie's bunny has floppy ears.
   The bunny finds pennies.

3. Molly's puppy hurries to see the bunny.
   The puppy smells plenty of daisies.

4. Twenty pretty kittens take a nap.
   Randy shows us a very sleepy kitty.

5. Molly's frisky puppy wants to play.
   The animals left a muddy mess.

6. Ronnie is hungry for toast and jelly.
   Everybody is happy about the party.

School–Home Connection
Ask your child to find all the words spelled with *y* or *ie* and read them aloud.

Name ______________________

▶ **Read the Spelling Words. Then write each word in the group where it belongs.**

Spelling Words

funny
happy
story
stories
hurry
hurried
how
out
baby
done

Words with y

Words without y

School-Home Connection

Have your child read each Spelling Word aloud. Ask your child to change *story* to make *stories*, and *hurry* to make *hurried*.

Name ______________________________

Write the word from the box that completes each sentence.

sunny	windy	family
worry	field	hurried

1. Angie and her ______________ went on a picnic.

2. They went to a grassy ______________.

3. It was a very ______________ day.

4. Then it got rainy and ______________.

5. They got their things and ______________ home.

Try This

Draw a picture of you and your friends having a picnic.
Use the words in the box to write about the picture.

School–Home Connection

Have your child read each completed sentence aloud. Ask him or her to tell which letters make the long e sound in *field* and *sunny*. (*ie, y*)

Name ___________________________

▶ Write a word from the box to complete each sentence.

great	took	poured	almost
traveled	blue	able	

1. Betsy's mom and dad ______________ her on a trip.

2. They ______________ to the seashore.

3. Betsy liked the sparkling ______________ water.

4. Betsy ______________ sand into a bucket.

5. Betsy was ______________ to swim with her mom's help.

6. It was a ______________ trip.

School-Home Connection

Have your child read the word *almost* from the box. Ask him or her to write the word in a sentence about a trip to the beach.

Name ______________________________

▶ **Read the story. Write three details about it.**

Jimmy likes to make things out of blocks. He makes a small house. He uses red blocks for the walls. Jimmy uses some black blocks for the windows. The beds are made from blue blocks. Jimmy plays for a long time. He is proud of all the things he made with blocks.

School–Home Connection

Read the story with your child. Ask him or her to read the parts of the story that are not details about what Jimmy is making. (*Jimmy plays for a long time; He is proud. . . .*)

Name ______________________________

▶ **Read the words in the box. Look at the pictures. Write the word that completes each sentence.**

daisies	families	happier
hurried	worried	prettiest

1. Julie was ______________ about her party.

2. "What if no one likes the ______________ on the cake?"

3. All the kids ______________ to see the cake.

4. They said it was the ______________ cake they had ever had.

5. That made Julie feel much ______________.

School-Home Connection

Ask your child to name the root word for each word in the box. *(daisy, family, happy, hurry, worry, pretty)*

Name ____________________

▶ **Change each verb in the box to a verb that tells about the past. Then choose one verb and write a sentence about the past.**

1.	jump	
2.	move	
3.	want	
4.	walk	
5.	clean	
6.	pick	

7. ____________________

School-Home Connection

Have your child tell you about what he or she did in school today. Encourage your child to use words that tell about the past. For example, *I watched the fish. I kicked the ball.*

Name ______________________________

Circle the sentence that tells about the picture.

1. The boy has two boats.
   The boy is in the room.
   The boy has on boots.

2. Jenny stands by the pole.
   Jenny goes to the zoo.
   Jenny has lost a tooth.

3. The owl fools the moon.
   The owl flew to the moon.
   The owl hoots at the moon.

4. This bird eats with a spoon.
   This bird eats fish for food.
   This bird sits on a stool.

5. Mom reads the news at noon.
   Mom reads a book.
   Mom reads to a poodle.

School-Home Connection

Ask your child to read each sentence aloud. Have him or her underline the words that have the vowel sound heard in *boot*.

Name ______________________________

▶ **Read the Spelling Words. Then write each word in the group where it belongs.**

Words with oo

______________ ______________

______________ ______________

______________ ______________

______________ ______________

____

____

Words without oo

______________ ______________

______________ ______________

______________ ______________

______________ ______________

____

____

Spelling Words

- boot
- tooth
- soon
- noon
- new
- grew
- story
- hurry
- great
- took

School-Home Connection

Have your child read each Spelling Word aloud. Write the words *book* and *booth*. Have your child change one letter in each word to make a Spelling Word (*took*, *tooth*).

Name ______________________________

Write the word from the box that completes each sentence.

blew	bloomed	roots	droopy
room	grew	noodle	cool

1. Oh, no! This plant looks ________________.

2. It may need more ________________ to grow.

3. I will water its ________________.

4. Now I'll put it in a ________________ spot.

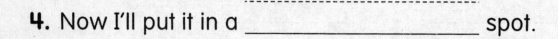

5. The plant ________________ so fast!

School-Home Connection

Ask your child to read each sentence aloud. Together, think of other words with the vowel sound spelled *oo* or *ew*, as in *bloom* or *grew*.

Name ______________________________

Write a word from the box to complete each sentence.

boy	building	tomorrow
toward	welcoming	

It's fun ______________ things out of clay. I like to make things with a ______________ named Carl. He has such a ______________ smile. When I carry my art ______________ the table, I will not drop it. I will finish this ______________.

Try This

Write your own sentence with the word <u>tomorrow</u>.

School-Home Connection

Have your child read each sentence aloud. Then talk about other ways your child could complete each sentence.

Name ______________________

Read the story about the picnic. Then answer each question.

Mom is taking my friends and me on a picnic. We are packing our food in a big cooler with some ice. Leslie and Mary pack ham and cheese sandwiches. Mom packs some apples. "Julie, don't forget to put in some water bottles!" Mom tells me. Now we are all set to go on our picnic.

1. What sandwiches will they eat? ______________________

2. What fruit will they eat? ______________________

3. Who is going on the picnic? ______________________

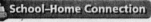

School-Home Connection

Have your child read the story to you. Talk about the items that are being packed for the picnic. What would your child pack?

Name ______________________________

Phonics: Contractions
'd, 've, 're, 's, n't, 'll
Lesson 29

▶ Complete each sentence. Write the contraction for the two words in the box.

I have

1. ______________ been here for a long time.

can not

2. I ______________ wait much longer.

They will

3. ______________ be late for the play.

She is

4. ______________ acting like a butterfly.

We are

5. ______________ going to a party later.

School-Home Connection

Write the following contractions: *you'd, you're, you'll.* Ask your child to tell you which two words each contraction stands for. (*you would; you are; you will*)

Name ______________________________

Write was or were on the lines to complete the story.

The house ____________ messy. It ____________ Mom's birthday. She ____________ still at work. Dad and Sandy ____________ cleaning. Arthur ____________ making a big cake. We ____________ excited. Soon the house and the cake ____________ ready.

Use was or were to write a sentence about what happened when Mom came home.

____

____

____

School-Home Connection

Encourage your child to use *was* to describe something that one person was doing, and *were* to describe something that two or more people were doing.

Name ____________________

▶ **Write the word from the box that completes the sentence.**

hold	kind	I'm
won't	tidy	open

1. "Can you ____________ the door?" asked Mom.

2. "____________ happy to help," said Joan.

3. "I'll be glad to ____________ some bags, too."

4. "That's very ____________ of you," Mom said.

5. "I ____________ forget how you have helped me."

Name ______________________

▶ **Read the Spelling Words. Then write each word in the group where it belongs.**

Spelling Words

find
mind
mild
cold
fold
most
soon
new
boy
building

Words with i

Words with o

Words without i or o

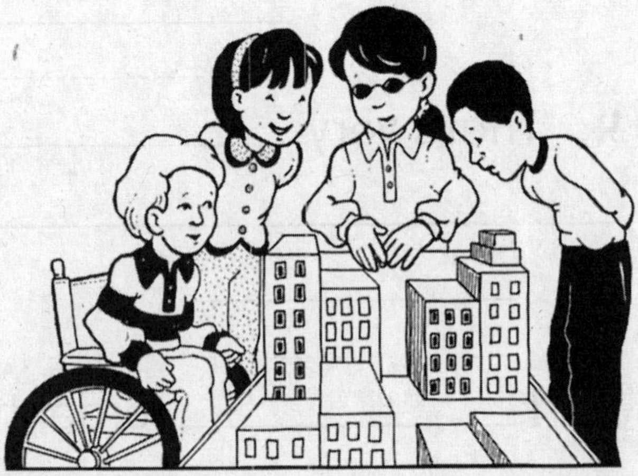

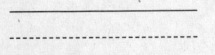

School-Home Connection

Have your child read each Spelling Word aloud. Write *kind* and *bold*, and have your child write Spelling Words that rhyme with each one.

Name ____________________

Write the word from the box that completes the sentence.

kind	chosen	behind
tiger	nobody	title

1. Janet had ____________ a book to read.

2. She liked the ____________ of the book.

3. The book was about a ____________.

4. It was the ____________ of book she liked to read.

Try This

Choose a word from the box. Write a sentence of your own.

School-Home Connection

Have your child read each completed sentence aloud. Ask him or her to write another sentence using one of the words from the box.

Name ______________________________

▶ **Finish the sentences to tell about yourself.**

1. When I get **ready** for school, I ______________________________.

2. I like to read **any** book that's about ______________________________.

3. I stand in the **front** of the mirror when I ______________________________.

4. There is **nothing** that I like more than ______________________________.

5. I say that I am **sorry** when I ______________________________.

School-Home Connection
Ask your child to read each sentence to you. Talk about what it means to be *ready*.

Name ______________________________

Each group of words is in ABC order.
Add more words. Keep the words in ABC order.

1. air	2. bridge	3. ______
4. ______	5. mall	6. ______

1. fine	2. ______	3. jail
4. ______	5. park	6. ______

1. ______	2. jungle	3. pond
4. ______	5. ______	6. zoo

School-Home Connection

Ask your child to make a list of six foods he or she likes to eat. Then ask your child to write the food words in ABC order.

Name ____________________

Read the clues. Then write the words where they belong in the puzzle.

holds	gold	sold
cold	old	fold

1. Mom ____ the baby.
2. It's not hot. It's ____.
3. My ring is made of ____.
4. I am 7 years ____.
5. I can ____ a shirt.
6. They ____ their house.

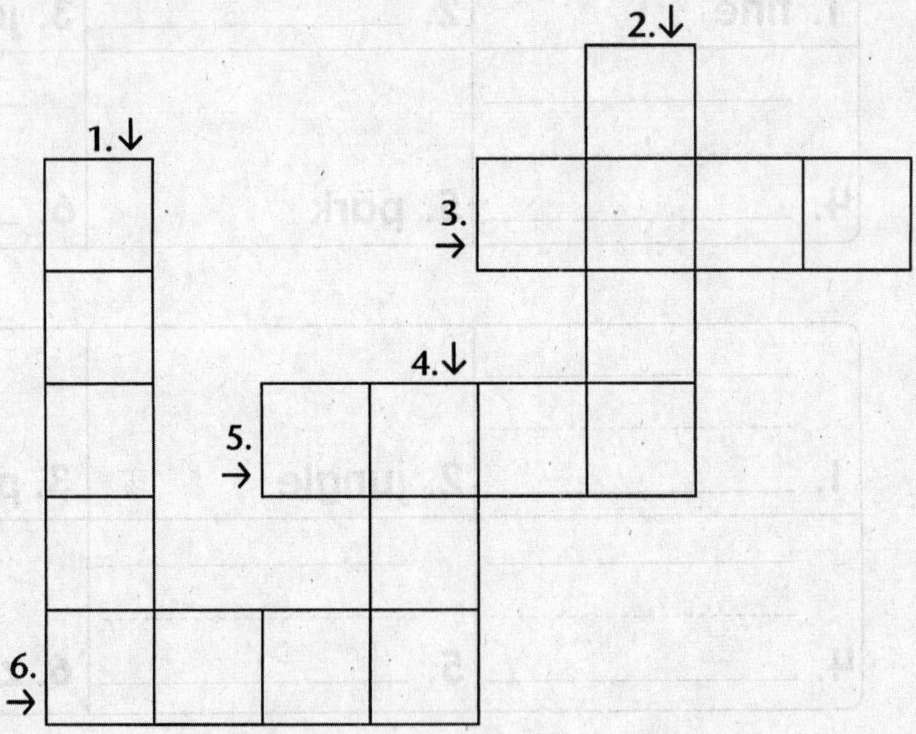

Name ______________________________

Write go and went to complete the story.

Planning the Party

Annie ________ to visit Liz last week. They ________ planned a party. Yesterday, Liz ________ to the store to buy milk and eggs. Today, Liz and Jan will ________ to Annie's house. They will make cupcakes.

Now, imagine you were invited to the party. Write a sentence to tell what you will do or what you did do. Use go or went correctly.

____

____

____

School–Home Connection

Talk about where you and your child went yesterday or last week. Then talk about where you will go today or tomorrow.

Cut-Out/ Fold-Up Books

Mule Brings News

"I have some bad news, little moles," said Mule.

"Why?" asked the moles. "What is this bad news?"

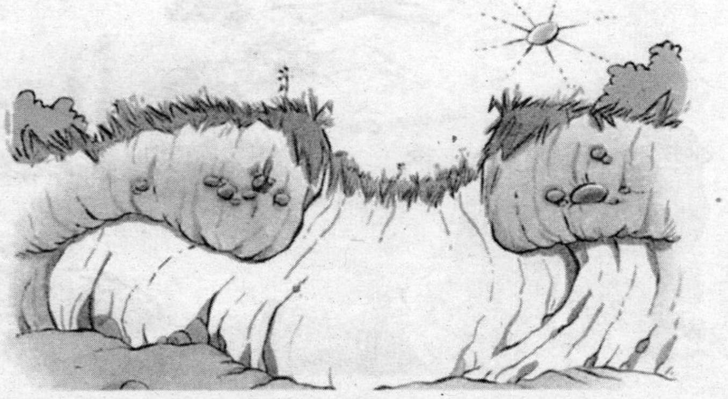

The moles jumped down into their hole. "Thanks for the news, Mule!" they called.

Fold

Fold

Mule spotted three cute moles beside a hole.

2

"The news is that a huge snake is coming," Mule told them. "Find a safe place to hide!"

7

Fold

"We don't want to hear bad news," the moles said.

4

Mule said, "I hate to be rude, but there is no time to waste!"

5

Fold

Little Bird found a

8 nice new home.

Little Bird flew for a long time.

6 The sky got lighter and brighter.

Fold

Little Bird's Flight

1

"I will fly around the earth!"

thought Little Bird. 3

Fold

Little Bird thought it
was time to fly away.

2

The days got longer
and warmer.

7

Fold

The winter was very cold.
Other birds flew along with her.

4

Sometimes there was very little
to eat. Little Bird was hungry.

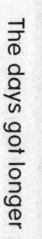

5

Fold

Bob Brown in Town

1

Bob made a list of things to buy. Then he went to town. 3

Fold

6 The friends shopped around town together. When they were done they went to Bob's house.

8 The friends ate a fine lunch together. "It's nice to have lunch with an old friend," said Rose. "It's nice to have lunch with my new friends," said a baby butterfly.

Fold

Bob Brown was hungry.
He wanted to eat.

2

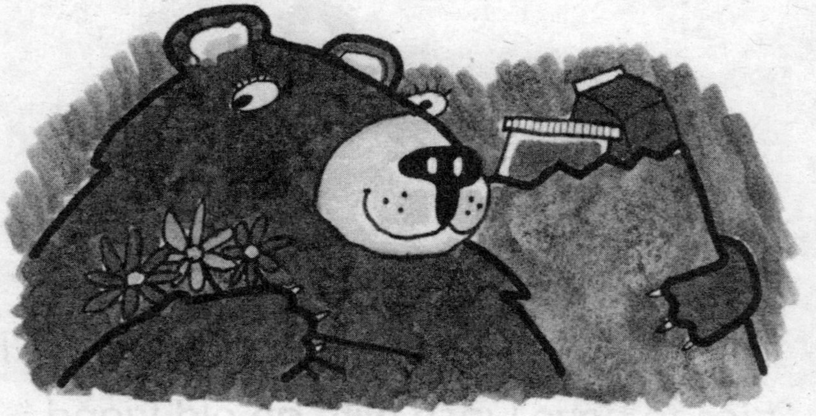

Bob Brown used the food to make
lunch. He even set out flowers!

7

Fold

In town, he met Rose. "I heard you
were in town," said Bob. "Can you
have lunch with me today?"

4

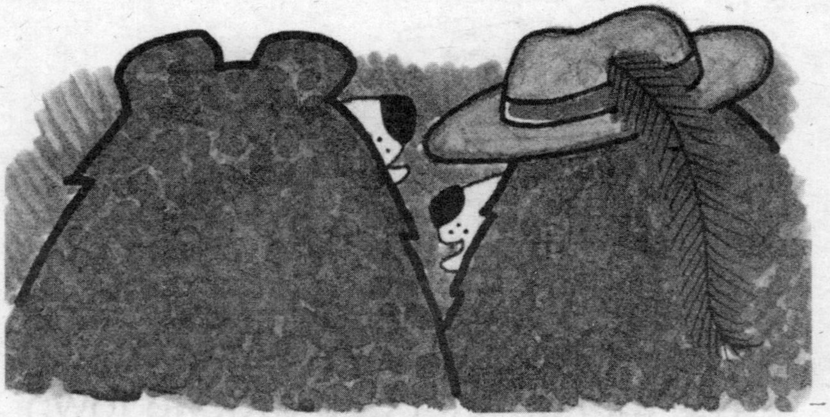

"Yes," said Rose. "How
nice of you to ask!"

5

Fold

Mike in the Sky

1

"Someday, I will be able to go up in the blue sky. I really want to try."

3

Mike dreamed that he got his wish. He got into a plane and took off!

6

Up in the blue sky, Mike wrote "I love to fly!"

8

Fold

Fold

Mike had a dream. He wanted to travel in a plane.

2

"This is great! It's easy! I can see trees and streams and fields!"

7

Fold

Mike went to school. He studied hard.

4

"Someday, I'm going to fly," he told his friends. "It's my dream."

5

Fold

At the Zoo

1

"Oh, boy! I am winning," she shouts.
Babs the baboon soon leads the way. 3

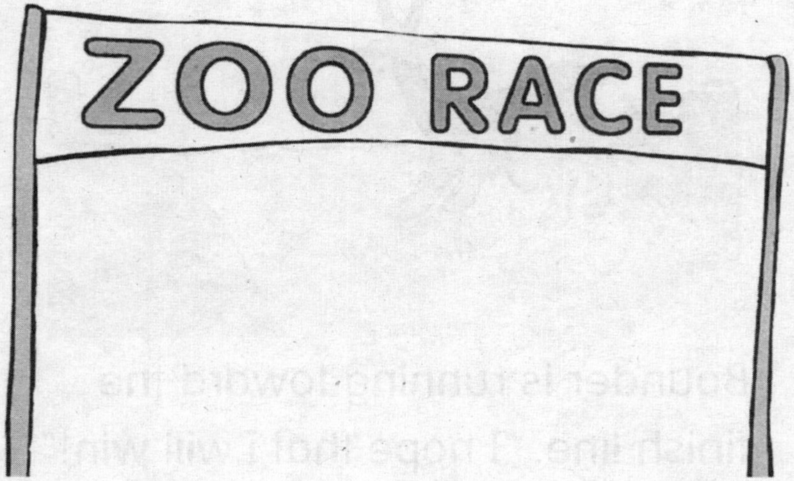

8 Who do you think will win?

Croc gets lost. "Oops! Now I won't finish the race until tomorrow!"
6 he says.

Fold

Fold

The welcoming sign is up.
It is time for the race.
"On your mark. Get set. Go!"

2

Fold

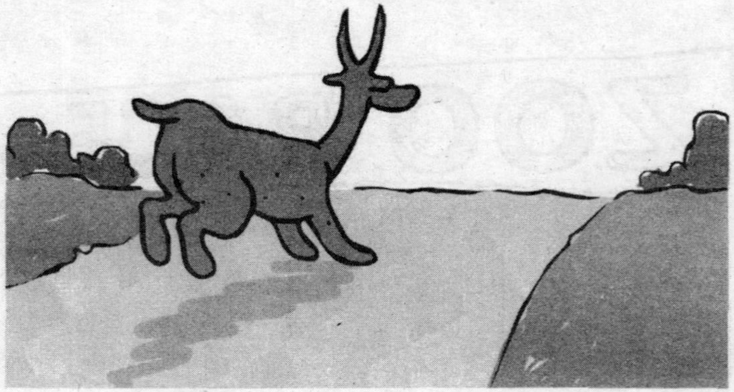

Bounder is running toward the
finish line. "I hope that I will win!"
says Bounder.

7

Ozzy runs like the wind. "I am
just a few steps away from
Babs," he says.

4

Fold

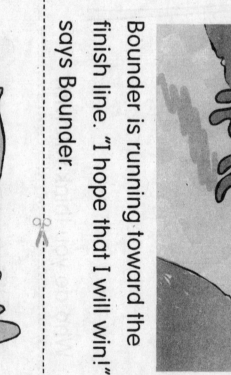

Richie is fast for his huge size.
The ground shakes as he runs.
"Here I come!" he calls.

5

8 What do you like to do on cold,
rainy days?

"Yes, I'm ready to help!"
6 Mom and I both like to bake.

Fold

What Can I Do?

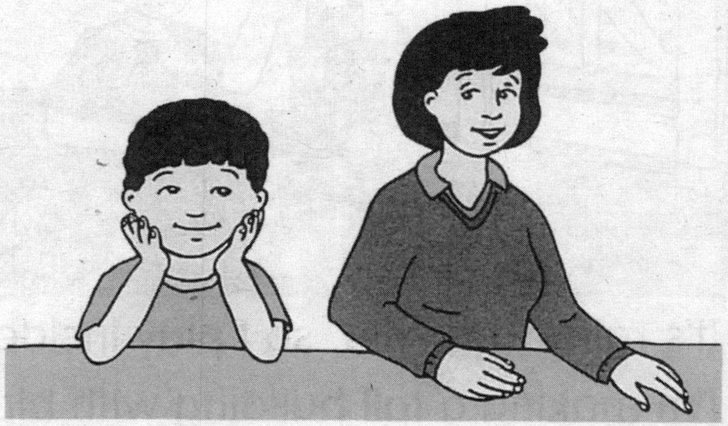

1

My building falls down. I don't want to play with blocks. There's nothing to play with!
"Find something new to do," says Mom. 3

It's rainy and cold, so I play inside.
I'm making a tall building with blocks.

2

This snack tastes really good! I hope it's cold and rainy tomorrow. Then we can bake again!"

7

Fold

I run like a wild animal. Mom says, "Don't run any more."
"I'm sorry," I say.

4

"Are you ready to help with the baking?" asks Mom.

5

Fold

The Thing Under the Bridge

Big Billy Goat
Middle Billy Goat
Little Billy Goat
Wind

Big Billy Goat: Look at the sun rise in the beautiful, blue sky.

Middle Billy Goat: Yes. It's a new day of eating grass.

Little Billy Goat: Today is just like yesterday. Tomorrow will be the same. Nothing ever changes.

Middle Billy Goat: Every day we eat grass and see the same things—

Big Billy Goat: the cool river,

Middle Billy Goat: the hill,

Little Billy Goat: the grass,

Big Billy Goat: the bridge,

Little Billy Goat: and all that yummy clover on the other side of the bridge.

Middle Billy Goat: If only we could cross the bridge.

Little Billy Goat: Why can't we cross the bridge?

Wind: Whoooooooooo! Whoooooooooooooo!

Big Billy Goat: Can't you hear that sound? That's why we cannot cross the bridge!

Little Billy Goat: I think you are just fooling around! That sound might just be the wind.

Wind: Whoooooooooo! Whoooooooooooooo!

Big Billy Goat: I think it heard you! Stand together so we will be safe!

Middle Billy Goat: It is very loud!

Big Billy Goat: Whatever it is, it must be big.

Wind: Whoooooooooo! Whoooooooooooooo!

Little Billy Goat: The clover looks great. I can almost taste it from here.

Big Billy Goat: Where are you going? I thought I told you we can't go!

Middle Billy Goat: Come back!

Big Billy Goat: Oh, dear! I can't look.

Middle Billy Goat: Is that Little Billy Goat walking toward the clover?

Big Billy Goat: No. It can't be.

Middle Billy Goat: He's climbing up the hill. I think he's eating the clover!

Big Billy Goat: Why is he rolling around on the ground like that?

Middle Billy Goat: I think he's very happy.

Big Billy Goat: That is not our Little Billy Goat. The thing under the bridge ate him all up!

Wind: Whooooooooooo! Whooooooooooooooo!

Middle Billy Goat: I don't think there is anything under the bridge!

Big Billy Goat: What?

Middle Billy Goat: I think it's only the wind!

Wind: Whooooooooooo!

Middle Billy Goat: I'm ready to go, too.

Big Billy Goat: Listen to me! Don't go! You will not be able to make it!

Middle Billy Goat: I'll see you on the other side!

Big Billy Goat: I see Middle Billy Goat on the other side of the river! He is jumping up and down. I know they are fine, but what about me? Look at those huge bites of clover! I'm going, too!

Wind: Whooooooooooo! Whoooooooooooooooo!

Big Billy Goat: Oh, no! The thing under the bridge will eat me!

Wind: Whooooooooooo! Whoooooooooooooooo!

Big Billy Goat: It does sound a lot like the wind.

Wind: Whooooooooooo! Whoooooooooooooooo!

Big Billy Goat: I see them waving to me again! They must be welcoming me to the other side of the bridge!

Wind: Whooooooooooo! Whoooooooooooooooo!

Big Billy Goat: Good-bye, Wind! I'm off to get some clover!

All Billy Goats: Hurray! We are all together again.

Little Billy Goat: The clover tastes great!

Wind: Whooooooooooo! Whoooooooooooooooo!

Big Billy Goat: I think the wind wants some, too!

Index

COMPREHENSION

GRAMMAR

HIGH-FREQUENCY WORDS

PHONICS

SPELLING

1-1: 3, 10, 17, 24, 31, 38 **1-2:** 3, 10, 17, 24, 31, 38 **1-3:** 3, 10, 17, 24, 31, 38 **1-4:** 3, 10, 17, 24, 31, 38 **1-5:** 3, 10, 17, 24, 31, 38